# Care and Repair
## Below Decks

*Some other books by the same author*

Build Your Own Boat
   (Stanley Paul Ltd.)

Practical Boatman
   (Stanley Paul Ltd.)

Small Boat Sailing
   (Macdonald Educational Ltd.)

Encyclopedia of Small Craft Maintenance
   (Pelham Books Ltd.)

Modern Sailmaking
   (Tab Books–U.S.A.)

Handbook of Practical Boat Repairs
   (Tab Books–U.S.A.)

Your Book of Knots
   (Faber and Faber)

Scouts on the Water
   (Scout Association)

Percy W. Blandford

# Care and Repair Below Decks

ADLARD COLES LIMITED
**GRANADA PUBLISHING**
London Toronto Sydney New York

Published by Granada Publishing in
Adlard Coles Limited

Granada Publishing Limited
Frogmore, St Albans, Herts AL2 2NF
and
3 Upper James Street, London W1R 4BP
Suite 405, 4th Floor, 866 United Nations Plaza, New York, NY 10017, USA
Q164 Queen Victoria Buildings, Sydney, NSW 2000, Australia
100 Skyway Avenue, Toronto, Ontario, Canada M9W 3A6
PO Box 84165, Greenside, 2034, Johannesburg, South Africa
61 Beach Road, Auckland, New Zealand

ISBN 0 229 11636 1

Printed in Great Britain by
Fletcher & Son Ltd, Norwich

Granada ®
Granada Publishing ®

# Contents

# Acknowledgements

All photographs and drawings are by the author except for the following:

Plates 11, 12, 13 and 14 were provided by Taylor's Para-Fin Oil & Gas Appliances Ltd.; plates 15 and 16 and figure 32 were provided by Blake & Sons (Gosport) Ltd.

# one

# Planning the work

Below decks are your living quarters, probably cramped by shore standards and sometimes a peculiar shape, but while you are afloat, this is your home. Your domestic comfort may be complicated and upset by the need to accommodate an engine or a centreboard case projecting into the living quarters, then sails and ropes, which may be wet and dirty, will sometimes have to be passed through the saloon. To complicate things further, your home cannot be relied on to remain upright, and on occasions it may get swamped with water.

Anyone with a little experience of boating offshore, or even on inland waters, will appreciate these points, but a beginner may approach the inside of a boat in a similar way to a home ashore and try to make the domestic quarters of his ship too much like a room of his house. There are certain things that just cannot be accepted afloat, so anyone new to boating is advised to delay the restyling of the accommodation with inappropriate things, such as unsuitable carpets or curtains or equipment that will not stand up to the damp and sometimes violent conditions afloat. It would be better to assume that whoever had the boat before found the accommodation satisfactory. Drastic alterations should be delayed until experience or the examination of other craft has shown what is feasible. This does not mean that a new owner should accept things just as they are, but he should use his own experience or that of others before tearing out and replacing and restyling any of the equipment or furnishings below decks.

The shape of a boat dictates how some things can be arranged, and there is a lot of skill in making the most of the bowl-shaped hull. In comparison, caravans are square boxes. There is much to be learned from the caravan industry, but what is possible in the simple shape of a caravan cannot always be adapted to a boat. There are some attractive caravan fittings, but before assuming that a lamp fitting, window frame or other piece of caravan equipment would have a use in your boat, make sure it will stand up to conditions afloat. An apparently brass item may be steel coated to look like brass. Aluminium caravan window frames may not be of a saltwater-resistant alloy. In both cases, corrosion might be rapid. However, anyone contemplating restyling the below-deck accommodation, may get some good ideas worth adapting by visiting a caravan exhibition.

To live comfortably in a confined space, it is essential to be as tidy as circumstances permit. This means that there should not only be a place for everything and everything in its place, but usually it should also be well secured. It is also more comfortable if the accommodation is clean and dry, as far as that is practicable. This usually means cleaning after a hectic passage. Oily finger marks from the voyage before last should certainly not be tolerated by a ship-proud owner. For comfort, the accommodation should be pleasant. This means lighter colours, particularly high up. The effect is to make a small place seem larger and more airy, even if ventilation at times is not as good as it should be. There is no place today for the Victorian idea of dark varnished wood everywhere. Dark colour low down may help to give a feeling of height and space to the lighter colour above. In a lightly built boat it also gives a feeling of solidity, which may help to pacify a nervous or seasick passenger.

Although care and maintenance should be an on-going thing, with work done as it becomes necessary, most owners give some time once a year to a more thorough attack on what needs to be done. The housewife calls it spring cleaning. We call it fitting out. It is at that time that alterations are usually made. They may be quite minor, but even then there may be sawdust scattered around and a risk of adjoining parts getting marked.

## Schedule

For this major spell of internal care and maintenance, it is as well to draw up a sequence of work that takes into account any alterations you intend to make. In general, repairs and alterations should be done before routine maintenance to parts which will not be altered. It is usually best to get dirty work out of the way first. If you want to clean out the bilges or make alterations there, it is unlikely that you will get through the work in confined spaces without transferring some of the dirt to other cleaner parts, so their cleaning should be left until later.

The conscientious owner carries a notebook and enters details of things to be done as he discovers them. These jobs and the routine maintenance jobs can be put in order, possibly at home away from the boat, but be prepared to modify your plan when you get to the boat and see something different from what you had visualised. If you are planning any work to be done inside the boat by professional help, it may be as well to get that done first, especially if it is to dirty things, like the engine or stern gear. Even a comparatively clean job, like fitting a new water tank or wiring in new instruments, may bring dirt or damage to something not directly involved. In the confined quarters of a boat it may be too much to expect that marking other parts can be avoided. If their maintenance is yet to be done, that may not matter very much, but it would be frustrating to have to do it a second time.

Anything that can be moved from the boat for cleaning, repair or alteration, should be taken out. This may include withdrawing screws from hinges so doors can be removed, making their maintenance easier and giving access to things beyond. It is always easier to work on a bench than to perform contortions to do the same job in a boat. You also get the opportunity to work on a removed part at leisure away from the boat. Even if all you have to do is clean or paint, you will usually make a better job of it then. Things like cookers and heaters can only be thoroughly cleaned and serviced if they are moved somewhere so that you can work more comfortably.

With the inside of the boat stripped of all that can be taken out, what is left will be as visible as it will ever be. If you are surprised by the amount of dirt revealed, that will show that

*Plate 1. There may be many interesting things to do on deck, but get below and put things in order there if you expect successful and trouble-free cruising.*

your efforts are justified. From this point onwards your activities should be aimed at doing all the maintenance necessary to the fixed parts before bringing back the removable items, unless you are planning alterations that involve the loose parts. Be careful to do comparable maintenance to fixed and removed items that should match. For instance, you may clean paintwork on a removed door so thoroughly at home that, when it is brought back to adjoin similar paintwork in the boat, which has had less effort spent on it, it will look several shades lighter.

There is something to be said for the policy of leaving well alone. If something is working satisfactorily, you will have to judge whether to open it up or not. You may have to get advice on how long an item may be expected to last. Something like the diaphragm of a pump may be working *now*, but will it last the season? If the part you are considering would make a mess if it had to be dealt with after all the things around it had been brought back into near showroom conditions, you may opt for a precautionary repair or service before it is due.

## Tools and materials

Besides planning the sequence of work, make sure you will have all you need at the time you need it. You may enjoy maintaining your boat, but that is no reason for getting frustrated as you plan to do a particular job and discover that tools or materials have been left at home or not even ordered. If you have to travel to your boat to work on it, give yourself an approximate work schedule, then list and take all you need to get through what you have planned. However, this is a hobby you are tackling for pleasure, so allow some time to eat and drink and even gossip. If the work takes longer or not as long as you estimate, it may not matter, but if you know what you intend to do and have all you need to do it, you will get more work done in a given time and feel more satisfied at the end of it.

Some guidance on the choice of tools is given in the chapters dealing with various materials.

## Condensation

It will be most unusual if your problems do not include condensation, and any attention to this should be given when much of the contents of the boat have been removed. In most cabin craft the accommodation is compact. Living space is much less than in your own home. It is usually smaller than in the average caravan, where condensation also has to be dealt with. Coupled with this is the complication of the casing around your living space being in close contact outside with the usually cold elements of air and water, while inside you want to keep warm. These are conditions that encourage condensation. If the temperature is the same both sides, condensation is much less or nonexistent.

When we breathe, we exhale moisture; our bodies are constantly giving it up; even the air contains it. It has to go somewhere. If it hits a cold barrier, it condenses. If it hits woven natural cloth it passes through the pores and gaps in the weave. If it hits woven synthetic fabric, there are no pores and not usually enough gaps to pass it so that the fabric becomes wet. If you sleep under a canvas cockpit cover or the cabin hatch opens under one, traditional cotton canvas may still be dry inside in the morning, while a synthetic cover may be running with moisture. This also applies to sleeping bags. Down in a cotton cover lets the

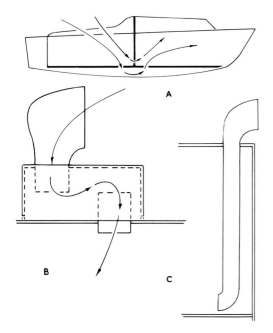

*1. Fresh air may be brought in through the sole (A) or taken low through a duct (C). Water can be kept out with the drained box of a Dorade ventilator (B).*

body breathe. Some synthetic fillings are barriers to dampness, but there are enough gaps in polyester and similar fillings to let body moisture pass. Synthetic covers to sleeping bags may seem desirable because of their resistance to water, but they will keep in body moisture and become unhealthily damp inside if not turned inside-out and aired daily.

## Ventilation

The best cure for condensation is ventilation, so the air inside is changed and at the same temperature as that outside. Obviously, this could be uncomfortable and we cannot accept it, but for other reasons besides condensation, the cabin should always be given as much ventilation as is acceptable and possible under particular circumstances. Ventilators of a type that cannot be closed should be built-in, in places where they are unlikely to admit water in rough conditions. In the best arrangement, air comes in low down then, as it is heated, it rises to pass out high up at a further part of the enclosed space.

Conditions are rarely ideal, but it may be possible to have ventilating grills low in the bulkhead next to the cockpit to let air in. It may also be possible to consider air coming in through the bilges, with air holes in the cabin sole or ventilators arranged in other parts that have air connections with the bilges (fig. 1A).

The outlet could be a cowled ventilator in the cabin top. An inland cruiser may have a simple arrangement, but for seagoing it should be a Dorade assembly to keep out water (fig. 1B and plate 2). Air flow low down in the cabin does not have to enter low. It may be better to use a cabin top ventilator and lead the air through a pipe to a low position (fig. 1C). This would avoid possible bilge smells in the cabin and be better than having air coming in as well as going out at cabin top level. Although the examples shown are single ventilators, it is usual to have

several to get a better circulation of air. The fixed ventilators can be supplemented with others that can be adjusted, but are available to give more air when it is needed.

## Insulation

As we often want the inside temperature higher than outside and only minimum ventilation may

*Plate 2. Dorade ventilators: ventilation without risk of water getting into cabin.*

be possible, condensation will occur. Under these circumstances it cannot be stopped, but its effect may be reduced. This is best done by an insulation gap between the outside and inside materials. To be fully effective the gap needs to be wide. Ideally it needs to be 5cm (2in) or more

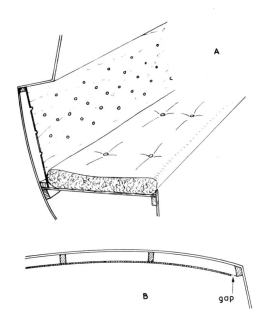

2. *Condensation can be minimised with a double thickness made by lining inside the hull or under the cabin top.*

plywood with a perforated pattern of holes would keep a sleeper away from condensation inside the hull (fig. 2A). If you can spare a slight loss of headroom and there are beams supporting the cabin top, a thin plywood lining could be fitted, but either leave gaps at the sides or perforate it, so that air can circulate in the space (fig. 2B). Something similar may be done at bulkheads: plywood can be held off with packings from fibreglass; doors may be thickened. You may not get 5cm, but any small amount will help. In all cases spaces could be filled with fibreglass insulation material or left with air circulating.

Paint manufacturers offer anti-condensation paints, such as International Korkon. These apply a coat of thickened absorbent material with a rough matt surface. Condensation enough to run is always more apparent on a glossy smooth surface than on a dull rough one. These paints do not prevent condensation, except to a limited extent, but they will absorb a night's moisture and they should be given a chance to dry out with plenty of ventilation every day, or as often as possible.

Condensation can also be caused by the heat generated by a person sleeping. If this can disperse, there is no problem, but where air circulation round the bunk is poor, dampness may build up. For example, if the bunk cushion rests on a solid plywood sheet, then either holes should be drilled in the wooden base (fig. 3A), or the plywood can be replaced with interlaced webbing (fig. 3B) which will incidentally improve comfort as well as

and can be just air or packed with an insulating material, such as fibreglass or plastic foam. We can learn from caravans, where this is done all round and condensation is no longer much of a problem. However, are you prepared to reduce the already small cabin by that much all round? Usually not.

Partial insulation may be possible. In many small craft the settee/bunks reach the hull. Thin

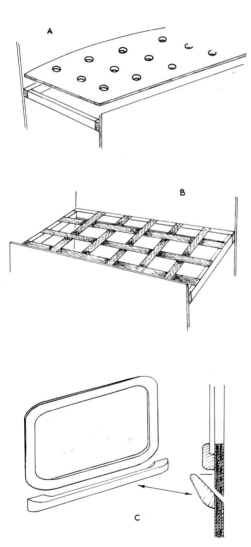

ventilation. If there has to be a solid support, put several layers of newspaper under the cushion or mattress, and dispose of it every day as it is likely to be quite wet in the morning.

Windows and portlights have their own condensation problems. Glass and acrylic will bring the cold through from outside and warm air will condense on the inner surfaces. Double glazing is not practicable. The condensation is often enough for water to run off the bottom and drop annoyingly if nothing is done to stop it. There may be a wood, plastic or metal channel that will have to be mopped out occasionally. If the window is high enough not to be within reach of waves, there could be a downward-sloping drain hole from the channel (fig. 3C).

*3. The underside of a bunk may be ventilated by a pattern of holes (A) or substituting webbing for a solid base (B). Condensation inside a window may be caught by a trough (C), with drain holes to the outside.*

# two

# Dealing with wood

Whatever the hull and main parts of the boat are made of, it is probable that many of the structures below deck will be wood. There is nothing like it for ease of working and making into individual assemblies, while it can be finished attractively and does not have the clinical appearance of plastic nor the austere look of metal. Certainly, for anyone wanting to make alterations or redesign the interior of a cabin, wood is usually the only satisfactory choice of material.

Almost any wood may be used internally in a boat, where it is protected from the worst effects of the weather and sea, but there are a few woods too prone to rot for use externally. It is advisable to avoid using these woods internally as well. The more resinous softwoods– which include most of the firs and pines–are safe to use. Some of the lighter softwoods, including Sitka spruce, chosen because of its lightness for spars, do not have a very long life unless well protected. Most of the hardwoods are safe choices, but there are exceptions, including birch and beech, which will not stand up to damp.

The choice of plywood to be used internally depends on its purpose. It should be made with a synthetic resin glue with a good resistance to moisture. Most plywood today has that type of glue. Some plywood for furniture use ashore is made of wood with little resistance to rot. The safest choice of plywood is the marine grade with the well known BSS1088 mark. An alternative is exterior grade, which may have similar outside veneers and the same glue, but there could be doubts about the quality of the inner veneers and the closeness of their internal edge joints. If the internal boat work is intended to have structural strength always use marine grade plywood, but something like divisions in a cabinet could be made from exterior grade. Exposed edges should be sealed with laminated or plastic strip.

## Protection and cleaning

Wood is a porous material that will absorb moisture and dirt. Teak and other naturally oily woods may have uses without treatment in some parts of a boat, but it is more usual to seal the surface in some way, both for protection and to improve appearance. Some furniture finishes used ashore are unsuitable afloat. French polish (shellac in methylated spirits or alcohol) will not withstand damp. Some synthetic sprayed furniture finishes are not damp-resistant. The more usual boat finishes are varnish and paint.

Painted or varnished surfaces inside a cabin should have quite a long life. It is unwise to consider stripping them, unless they have suffered considerable abuse. If the only trouble is dirt, washing may be the only treatment needed; this could be done with cold fresh water (not salt water) wiped over with a cloth. If this is unsuccessful, try warm water, then try warm water with soap or go on to a synthetic detergent. Avoid too much heat or too great a concentration and do not leave it on too long, or the surface of the paint or varnish may be softened.

If these comparatively mild treatments do not work, try a domestic solvent on local bad spots.

You could try a dry cleaning fluid, such as carbon tetrachloride in one of its proprietary forms. With any of these solvents, follow with enough clean water to flow surplus solvent away, then wipe with a damp cloth and leave to dry; too long a treatment may soften the finish. Avoid domestic scouring powders; they may clean but, despite what may be said on the container, they are abrasive and may remove gloss. A cleaning mixture used by antique furniture restorers will get through dirt and dissolve wax and furniture polish; this is made of equal parts of vinegar, paraffin and methylated spirits.

Sugar soap is the oldtime paint cleaner for wooden boats. It is powerful and rough on the skin; and is usually more powerful than is needed on cabin woodwork; if you have to clean the inside of the hull, follow the maker's directions and use plenty of water to pump it out of the bilges.

If any part of the woodwork has been rubbed bare, it should be repainted or varnished, but avoid a hard edge on the old surface by sanding around the damage. Wet-and-dry abrasive paper used damp is best, but ordinary glass-paper of medium (M2) grade is cheaper. As the latter does not usually have waterproof glue, warm it before use to drive off any moisture in the glue, and it will last longer.

*Painting*
Paint for touching up ought to be used in the same sequence as the original painting, which was probably primer, undercoat and top coat; but for a small repair, two or three applications of top coat will do. If you can match the colour, that is fine, but otherwise it may be better to repaint the whole thing after touching up the damage. In that case the gloss should be taken off, either by rubbing with fine abrasive paper or by scouring. A domestic scouring powder on a damp cloth will do it, but pumice powder may be better. Fine steel wool will also take off gloss, but make sure all particles are removed, or they will cause rust marks in the new finish.

Varnish can be treated in the same way as paint, and there should be little difficulty in matching colour if you use a marine grade–as you should. If the part that has been rubbed bare has been neglected and has absorbed dirt, try wiping it with domestic bleach, but follow with clean water and let it dry before varnishing.

If a varnished surface is sound but dull or with an uneven gloss, there is an alternative to rubbing it down and applying another coat of varnish. Use a paste or spray furniture polish. Modern ones that contain silicone do not need rubbing.

*Polishing*
Some internal woodwork may have a wax polished finish. The wood was almost certainly sealed with a couple of coats of varnish or sealer, which were rubbed matt and then waxed. If you have to deal with a bare wood part, treat that in the same way. If you try wax only, you will work hard and never achieve a match.

Buy proper furniture wax polish, which is a mixture of beeswax and the harder carnauba wax; it is no use trying to use the ball of beeswax you may have for pulling sail twine through. You cannot achieve a wax polish if there is no wax there, which may seem obvious, but you must put on one or two coats with the minimum of rubbing so that a layer is built up before giving a hard rub. Put wax on with a fairly absorbent dry cloth, but for the final finish you may get a better result with coarser stuff; even a piece of hessian. A gap of a day or so between coats gets a better result.

If you have to deal with teak that has either been left bare or treated with oil, do not attempt to varnish or even wax it. Dirt may have been absorbed by the applied or natural oil, and water will not shift this, so use a solvent. Degreasing fluid will do it, but a cloth soaked in paraffin or methylated spirits may be just as effective. For a stubborn patch use carbon tetrachloride, but wipe that off before it soaks in.

For teak there are special oil mixtures, which may be sold as teak oil or tung oil. They are wiped on and most do not have to be rubbed. The effect is to revive the appearance of the teak and leave it with a satin surface that will resist marking. Periodic treatment as the surface shows signs of deteriorating will restore a good appearance.

## Minor surface damage

There are some furniture restorers' ideas that may work on marked varnish, oil or waxed finishes. White rings caused by hot or wet cups may disappear with furniture polish. Metal polish can be used on them and cigarette ash mixed with water acts in the same way. On varnished mahogany, wipe with linseed oil and rub with half a Brazil nut.

If the surface finish is scratched, without going through to the wood, polishing may be all that is needed. If there is dirt in a scratch, either remove it with a solvent or poke it out, otherwise polishing will make it look darker.

If the finished wood has suffered a blow, so there is a hollow in it, this may be removed by a furniture restorer's method if the surface can be brought horizontal. Put some water in the hollow, then heat an old spoon almost to redness and put it in the water. This will generate steam which will enter the wood and expand the compressed fibres.

If a scratch or cut goes through the finish and damages the wood, a filler is advisable. Plastic wood has possibilities, particularly if the damage is such that some of the wood has gone. When plastic wood has set it can be carefully cut and sanded so it may be built up to replace missing slivers of the original; but this has limited application. If there is much wood missing, you will have to let in another piece. If all you have to do is fill a crack or hole, a stopping is more appropriate. Some furniture stoppings are not waterproof. One intended for boats is Brummer Waterproof Stopping, obtainable in colours to match several woods.

## Screwing

Screws which have loosened may need attention.

The simplest treatment is to withdraw the screw, push a matchstick in the hole and drive the screw again. In some cases a thicker screw of the same length can be used or a longer screw of the same gauge can be driven if there is enough thickness of wood. Sometimes a fitting can be moved slightly so new holes may be drilled. It is advisable to plug the old holes to prevent the voids loosening nearby screws, even if they will be hidden by the fitting. Plugs can be roughly shaped and cut off with a chisel used bevel downwards (fig. 4A).

If the screw has to remain in the same place, the hole may be drilled out to take a plastic or fibre wall plug, which should be punched slightly below the surface (fig. 4B), so any expansion upwards does not lift the fitting. A piece of dowel rod may be used in the same way, but that puts the screw into weaker end grain. A better use for dowel rod is in a place where something like the weight of a hanging door has caused loosening. Then it is put crosswise for the screw to penetrate (fig. 4C).

Another way of securing a screw is to fill the hole with a mixture of glue and sawdust, then drive the screw into that; pressure may have to be kept on until the glue has set. If you think the screw may have to be withdrawn at some future date, use a water-resistant glue (Aerolite 306 or Cascamite). If you use epoxy (Araldite) it will adhere to the screw, and attempts at withdrawal will sever wood fibres, so only use that if permanency is what you want.

## Manufactured boards

Hardboard and chipboard are increasingly used ashore and they have limited uses for cabin work. Most hardboard is about 3mm thick, with one hard smooth surface and the other patterned. The type that should be considered for boat work is that described by the makers as 'oil tempered' or some similar name, because only this is sufficiently water-resistant. Perforated and fluted or otherwise decorated boards are not oil-tempered, so they cannot be used for cabin lining and similar purposes. The smooth surface should always be outwards and it should not be broken by sanding. Hardboard is absorbent, so that a sealer for use with it should be used before painting or varnishing, otherwise a large number of coats will have to be applied to get a good final surface. If the reverse side is not otherwise protected, give that and the edges the same treatment as the front, even if they will not show. It can be cut and drilled like wood. It will take wood glue on the back, but if the front is to be glued, it should be sanded matt at the joint.

Chipboard, made of particles of wood bonded together with synthetic resin, is being increasingly used as a wood substitute ashore. Although it is unacceptable for building a boat, it has possibilities inside. It makes good work tops in the galley and may be bought with plastic-covered surfaces. While it may be worked like wood, it does not take wood screws very well. Screws with special threads for chipboard are only made of steel, so are unsuitable for use afloat as they rust. It is better to plug the

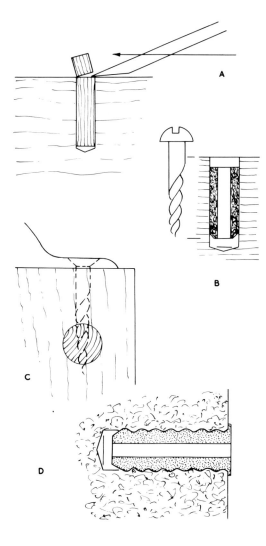

material and drive brass screws into the plugs. Plugs intended for walls might be used, but there are special chipboard plugs obtainable (fig. 4D).

## Tools

An enthusiastic woodworker can accumulate a large collection of tools and today many of these are power driven, each with its built-in motor. Obviously, any tools already owned will be useful for boat work, but jobs that have to be done away from home may be out of reach of electric power, and if tools have to be transported there is an advantage in those that are compact and may have more than one use. The following notes are intended as a guide to the choice of tools for hand work in repair and alterations. For work that can be done ashore, a substantial bench and vice with several power tools are worth having.

Many cuts on wood have to follow curves, and a pad saw will do most of this. You should have three blades: the largest wide blade will do general work, while the two narrower blades will follow sweeping curves. The smallest has a narrow end so that it can be pushed through a hole to make internal cuts. The teeth of all three blades tend to be coarse. For smoother cuts, particularly across the grain, when making

*4. A loosened screw may have its hole drilled out and plugged (A) or a wall plug can be sunk in a hole (B). A screw into end grain will get a better grip through a dowel (C). Special plugs are made for screwing into chipboard (D).*

joints or cutting wood to fit closely, there is no
substitute for a tenon saw, with teeth no coarser
than 14 per inch. Another useful cheap tool is a
coping saw, with some spare blades. This has a
sprung frame which tensions the narrow blade,
and will cut any shape down to quite tight
curves (fig. 5A), being particularly useful on
plywood.

Any available hammer may do all the hitting
you want, but if you buy one, get a claw hammer
(fig. 5B). The divided claw is intended for pulling nails, but it will also serve as a crowbar, for
levering things apart. Pliers will also serve as
pincers for pulling nails; have the type with
cutters, then you can get the cutter jaws under
a nail head and lever it up. Traditionally, a
mallet is preferred to a hammer for hitting wood
or chisels, but you can use a hammer over a
scrap of wood for knocking joints together, and
plastic chisel handles stand up to quite rough
treatment.

*Chisels and planes*
Chisels are better with bevel edges than with
square edges as they will get into tighter angles
(fig. 5C). If you do much woodwork you may
feel that you never have as many chisels as you
need, but 6mm ($\frac{1}{4}$in), 12mm ($\frac{1}{2}$in) with one quite
wide one about 40mm ($1\frac{1}{2}$in) will make a start in
your kit to take afloat. Some chisels come with

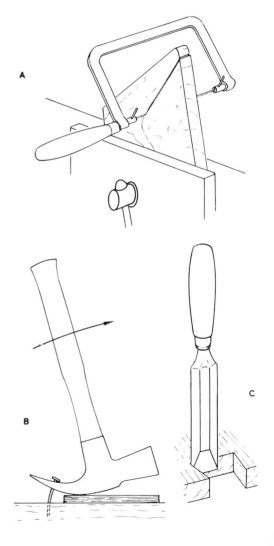

*5. A coping saw is useful for the many curves in
wooden boat parts (A). A claw hammer (B) can be
used for levering as well as drawing nails. A bevel-edged
chisel will do all that a square-edged one can and get
into corners less than a right-angle.*

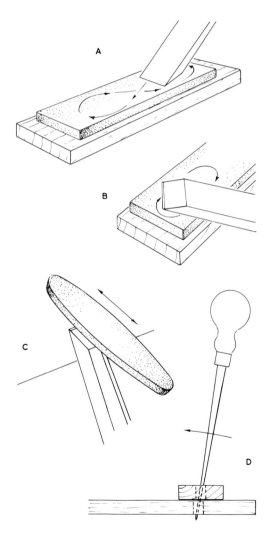

plastic covers to go over the cutting edges. Chisels have to be kept sharp if they are to be any good, so look after them.

Planes may be reduced to one as most work can be done with a steel smoothing plane, such as a Stanley or Record no. 4, if you also have one or two Surform tools. These have pierced steel blades, that can be replaced when blunt, and they may be flat or curved. The filing action of these tools is easier to manage in awkward situations than conventional planing.

Chisels, planes and other edge tools have to be kept sharp. The device for this in the work-shop is an oilstone (fig. 6A and B); afloat you may take a flat scythe stone and use it with water. Water and oil do not mix, so you cannot change lubricants on a stone. The flat scythe stone has an oval shape with flat sides and you can either rub the tool on it or use it like a file on the steel (fig. 6C).

*Drills*

If you do not have power aboard, drilling may be done with a hand drill (wheel brace) for screws and anything up to 6mm. You can push a bradawl in for the smallest screws, and a pointed ice pick is useful for marking centres for drilling, making small holes, or levering holes into line (fig. 6D) as well as for rope

6. *The sharpening bevel of a chisel or plane iron is made by rubbing at a constant angle all over an oilstone (A), followed by rubbing the other side flat (B). A flat scythe stone can be used on an edge like a file (C). An awl or ice pick has several uses, including pulling holes into line (D).*

splicing and breaking ice into the ice box. Metalworking twist drills do not make clean holes in wood and for holes over 6mm ($\frac{1}{4}$in) it is better to use a carpenter's brace; as many holes in a boat are in places where a full sweep cannot be taken, get one with a ratchet. Fast-cutting centre bits, with screwed points are good general purpose bits. Unfortunately, you need one for each size hole, but 12mm ($\frac{1}{2}$in) and 19mm ($\frac{3}{4}$in) are your most likely needs. It is possible to get expansive bits (Irwin) for holes over 19mm ($\frac{3}{4}$in) up to mast hole size, but whether the expense is justified depends on your needs.

A 'rose' countersink bit may fit the wheel brace and deal with the tops of screw holes, but a larger one for a carpenter's brace will clean the mouths of larger holes. Get a screwdriver bit for the carpenter's brace. It will tighten stubborn screws and withdraw others that defy the normal screwdriver. Although ratchet and pump-action screwdrivers are attractive, plain screwdrivers with long blades and oval handles are more use afloat.

*Other tools*
Wood will usually have to be gripped by improvising holds, sitting or kneeling on it. There are portable vices to cramp on to anything convenient, and a plank across the cockpit will serve as a bench for one of these. G-cramps are useful for holding wood being worked on and pulling parts together; sizes are quoted by the maximum opening. Not all makes close completely in the larger sizes, but if you can get

23cm (9in), two of these will cope with most work. Otherwise you may have to get a 10cm (4in) or 15cm (6in) as well, for the sake of its closure on thin material. Packing blocks are usual, so gaps can be made up.

Synthetic resin glues are best applied by using disposable equipment. A tapered piece of wood with a broad chisel-like end (fig. 7A) is better than a brush for spreading. If you use a two-part glue, tie cloth around the end of a stick to apply the acid hardener (fig. 7B). Do not nail it on or use a brush with metal binding, as the metal may cause staining of the glue line. Plastic containers are useful for mixing glue for immediate use, but some glues will eat their way through some plastics. If glue is to be kept, put it in a glass jar.

If you will be painting or varnishing during a work session, make sure you have made provision for looking after the brushes. They are too valuable to discard. If you know a brush will be needed again soon, immersing the bristles in water until tomorrow seems to work, even if the experts disagree; it might be better to use thinners instead of water. Water, however, will shake off whereas thinners have to be dried away thoroughly or they will affect the viscosity of the next coat. When you have finished with a brush, clean it with thinners or solvent (Polyclens) followed by detergent and warm water and a rinse in clean water.

*Measuring*
Most of us possess an expanding rule. This has taken over from the many-fold carpenter's rule,

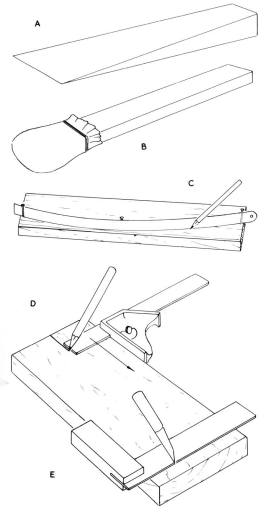

but it is worthwhile having a straight steel rule, as much for drawing lines, including curves (fig. 7C), and testing levels as for measuring. A normal set-square is useful for marking and checking right-angles, but if you buy a tool, a combination square is better. This has a sliding head on a stiff rule and can be used for angles of 45 degrees as well as 90. Probably its greater advantage afloat is that you can reduce the

*7. Glue may be spread with a wedge-shaped piece of wood (A). Hardener is spread with cloth tied on a stick (B). A steel rule can be used for drawing curves (C) as well as for measuring. An adjustable square can be used as a marking gauge (D). Mark lines for cuts with a knife (E).*

*8. An adjustable bevel has frequent uses for marking and testing the variety of angles on a boat.*

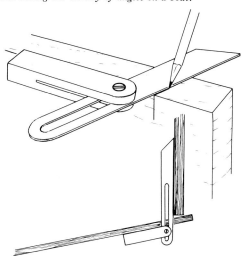

length of its blade to get into awkward places and, with a pencil against the end of the rule, you can draw the tool along to mark a distance parallel to an edge (fig. 7D). Precision cuts are best marked with a knife–any knife–there is no need to buy a special one (fig. 7E). There is a craftsman's saying about 'measuring twice before cutting once'. It is very appropriate to fitting pieces of wood into a boat.

Many cuts are not at right-angles. An adjustable bevel is a simple and essential tool for marking and checking them (fig. 8). It is more useful to a boatbuilder than to other woodworkers.

# three

# Dealing with plastics

The rapid development of satisfactory plastics was one of the good things that came out of World War II, and in the years since then they have revolutionised many aspects of boat-building. Most obvious is the use of fibreglass, but in many parts of a boat and its equipment there are things made of plastic that would once have been made of wood, metal, rubber or other natural material. There is a considerable variety of plastics, and methods of treating them vary. Unfortunately, they are not easily identified and there may have to be some trial and error when dealing with repair or altera-tions, to discover if it is possible to bend, stick or melt the particular material.

The terms 'plastic' and 'synthetic' are usually interchangeable as most plastics used afloat are man-made, but for convenience I have left consideration of those soft materials often called 'synthetics' or 'man-made fibres' until the chapter on fabrics, and only the harder plastics are dealt with here.

The finish on wood is an applied one, and any gloss or polish is on the applied film of paint, varnish or wax. The finish on plastic is the smoothness of the material itself. There is no such thing as absolute smoothness, but what we consider a smooth surface has scratches so fine that they are not normally visible.

If a plastic surface has become scratched or otherwise damaged or if there is a need for reviving the overall surface, treatment is with successively finer abrasives. The degree of coarseness of the first step depends on the state of the surface.

## Polishing

If there are scratches to be removed, it may be necessary to file the surface, but much can be done with a woodworking scraper or a knife dragged sideways–and this has the advantage of not making coarse scratches that would have to be removed. Avoid the darker abrasives, such as emery, which would discolour lighter plastics. Glasspaper or garnet paper are suitable, or the manufactured abrasive paper often called wet-and-dry. This last is graded according to the grits per square inch, but there are traditional marks for the other materials as shown on page 26. It should not usually be necessary to start with anything coarser than 100 grit (or equivalent), then go to 120 or 150. For shaped parts it may be easier to use loose grit on a cloth. An alternative to the finer grit is pumice powder or household scourer on a damp cloth. Steel wool may be used, but this should be the type obtainable graded in fineness and not the household cleaning type.

Each grade of abrasive must completely re-move the scratches made by the previous grade, then any grit left on the surface should be wiped off, otherwise contaminating a later grade with particles from an earlier one will spoil the surface. It helps to change direction to see if earlier scratches are removed.

For the finishing stages there are finer abrasives that the makers would rather call polishes or cutting compounds. There are some intended to finish newly-sprayed car paint, but brass polish followed by silver polish, after a fine powder or paper abrasive, should put a high gloss on most plastics. When there is just a general dullness of a plastic surface, one of these last treatments should revive it.

There are a few plastics that are soft despite their rigidity. If they do not respond to graduated stages of abrasive and their surface has become unattractive, they can be brightened by treating as wood with a furniture polish sprayed or rubbed on. These plastics are often used for the cases of instruments. Protect the transparent front of the instrument before polishing in this way or its surface may be damaged when removing sprayed polish from it. Masking tape is useful for this protection.

*Acrylic*
Acrylic or Perspex (Plexiglass) is made in coloured and transparent forms. Windows of boats are often made of it. When new, its transparency is supposed to be about $1\frac{1}{2}$ times as good as glass, but this depends on the polish of the surfaces. As the material is not very hard, some abrasion must be expected. Deep scratches would have to be removed in the way described for other plastics, but rubbing away much of the surface would make it uneven, so the view would be distorted. However, more light would come through.

To deal with dulling of acrylic surfaces, whether clear, translucent or opaque, the makers usually offer two polishes, to be used in sequence to restore a shine. Without them, the first stage could be fine pumice powder on a damp cloth, followed by silver polish. Do not use window-cleaning fluids or sprays.

## Altering plastics

If anything made from plastics has to be altered or repaired there is a certain amount of luck concerning what work is possible. If it is a hard substance that has obviously been moulded or cast, it will probably be brittle. This would be identified as a part with double curves and possibly a patterned shape or raised lettering. Treat this cautiously if you want to cut it or do other work on it. If the plastic appears to have started as a sheet, as it would for a panel, screen or window, you can expect it to be more amenable to working with tools. There are some moulded plastics that are not fully hard and have a quality like stiff rubber. These may not crack, but they are difficult to work satisfactorily with such tools as saws and drills. With any plastic article that you want to repair or alter, it is a safe rule to keep to hand tools. The heat generated by a power tool may soften the plastic to a point where it melts or disintegrates. For instance, a quick cut across a piece of Perspex with a bandsaw may soften it so much that the edges melt together again behind the saw.

If plastic is to be sawn, use a fine-toothed saw slowly with many teeth in contact and the plastic supported close to the cut. To get maximum contact, use the saw at a flat angle (fig. 9A). A Junior hacksaw should work better than a woodworking saw. It is possible to plane a straight edge sometimes, but it has to be done with a steel plane having a narrow mouth. Usually is better to file the edge and finish it with abrasive paper wrapped around a block of wood.

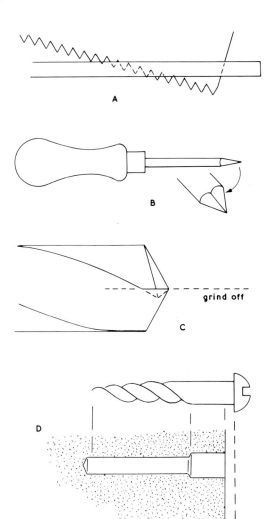

A

B

grind off

C

D

If it is an exposed edge, you can follow with a polishing sequence.

*Drilling and screwing*
Drilling is the process most likely to cause breakages. Do not use a centre punch, but a dent can be made with an awl filed to a triangular point (fig. 9B), twisted in the hand. For holes up to about 3mm (⅛in) ordinary metalworking twist drills used in a hand wheel brace should make a clean job. For larger holes the ordinary drills tend to snatch and pull so they crack the plastic. There are special drills with steeper flutes, but you can adapt a metalworking bit by grinding its leading edges upright (fig. 9C). Have the other side of the plastic supported and put on only enough pressure to keep the drill cutting.

Much screwing to plastic ashore is done with self-tapping screws, but as these are steel and will rust, they are inadvisable afloat; instead you can use brass wood screws. However, if part of the unscrewed neck has to go into the plastic, as it would when fixing a thin piece of metal, drill a clearance hole for the depth the neck would go (fig. 9D), otherwise the mouth of the hole will be cracked. The tapping hole for the threaded part should be fairly generous in

*9. When sawing plastic, keep many teeth in contact by sloping the saw (A). Use an awl with a square point for marking centres of holes (B). A larger drill can be prevented from snatching and breaking plastic by grinding its cutting edge vertical (C). For a screw into plastic there should be clearance for its neck and a tapping hole deeper than its thread (D).*

diameter and rather deeper than the screw will go. If you are working in warm conditions go ahead and drive the screw. Most plastics are more brittle when cold than hot. If you have any doubts, warm the screw before driving it slowly–get it almost too hot to hold and it will soften the plastic as it goes in.

Unfortunately there is no universal adhesive for plastics. For some there is no satisfactory way of sticking them. Many plastic parts, both hard and soft, are made of poly vinyl chloride (PVC); tube adhesive for this is obtainable. The instant adhesives have possibilities for some plastics, but follow directions and avoid getting any on your hands. 'Clear Bostik' will stick some plastics. For acrylic the makers supply an adhesive which melts the surfaces into a weld, but take care not to get any where it is not wanted, as it will spoil the smoothness of the surface. Although epoxy glues stick almost anything, there are a few plastics that will not take them. Trial is the only real test. Almost all adhesives, except its own specially developed preparation, eat away polystyrene foam (often used as buoyancy or insulation material).

If a crack develops, but does not go right across, it can be stopped by drilling quite a small hole at its end, but make sure it really is the end (fig. 10A).

### Bending

Not many plastics can be bent satisfactorily, but acrylic is one that can be softened with heat and bent into almost any shape. Unfortunately, the surface can be damaged at this stage. If you

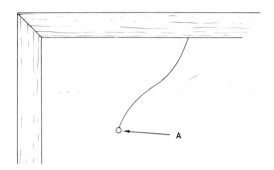

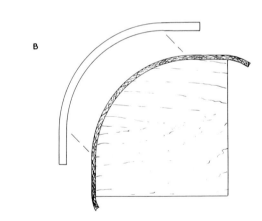

*10. A crack in a plastic panel can be stopped with a small hole (A). Heated perspex may be bent around a padded former (B).*

can manipulate it to the shape you want without the surfaces touching anything, that is fine, but if you want to bend around a former there must be something on the surface of it to prevent damage to the Perspex. Chamois leather is best. Cloth would transfer the pattern of its weave to the soft plastic.

Do not try compound curves. They are made in industry, but with simple equipment a bend or twist should have straight lines across; allow some excess at the ends for handling. A simple example is a piece of clear or coloured transparent Perspex bent into a lamp shade (fig. 10B).

Some clear acrylic will soften in boiling water, but most obtainable now and all the coloured types need more heat than that. Put the plastic in a domestic oven and heat it until you can pick it up with leather gloves and find it as limp as cloth. Drape it over the mould, without pressing the surface. Hold the ends until enough heat has gone for the material to retain its shape. It can then be cooled in water. Beware of heating vacuum-formed plastics. These will quickly return to their original flat sheet condition, as anyone knows who has tried pouring hot liquid into an empty margarine container.

Other plastics that may not soften enough to bend and keep a shape unaided, may be softened with hot water, then sprung and held to a curve by screwing. The plastic used for hoses is much more workable when warm. If a hose has to push over a metal pipe, soak hose and pipe in hot water and push together before they cool. Even if the metal cannot be heated, the warm plastic hose should go on. It would be helpful to enlarge the end of the hose with a wooden fid just before pushing it on to the nozzle or pipe—not a metal spike, as that would take away the heat.

Most cold plastics will be unmarked if held between wooden vice jaws; fibre clamps provided with some metalworking vices should also be safe, otherwise use wood or scrap flat plastic as padding. Do not use any more pressure than necessary in a vice or any sort of cramp. Putting under weights may be a better way of holding a glued joint together; small jobs can be held with clothes pegs.

## Tools

Some tools have been mentioned already, and most working in hard plastic is a compromise between woodworking and metalworking techniques. Metalworking files will shape edges, but the marks they leave will have to be removed with progressively finer abrasives. If the edge can be pared with a chisel or a finely-set plane, the surface will be smoother and not so much work with abrasives will be needed.

Although a 'Junior' hacksaw is the best tool for sawing without cracking plastic, its scope is limited. For a long cut parallel to an edge, a full-size hacksaw with the finest blade you can find and set crosswise may be used, with the sheet held down overlapping the edge of the bench by the minimum amount.

### Laminated plastics
The edges of laminated plastics (Formica etc.) can be filed or planed. In both cases the tool must cut away from the top surface, or that may chip or break out (fig. 11A). There are special tools that work with a plier action to nibble this

material to any outline, but it is possible to get the shapes with saws and files. There is another tool to trim the edge to the usual slight bevel, instead of using a file or plane; these are not worth getting, especially for the small amount of laminated plastic in most boats.

If new laminated plastic is to be put on a plywood or chipboard working top, it should be fixed with a contact adhesive. It has to be positioned correctly first time. Spreading of the adhesive must be complete and with a thin even coat. This is done with a tool made of steel with a coarse saw-tooth edge (fig. 11B), pulled across the adhesive as soon as it has been poured. If the top has suitable edges, temporary stop pieces can be nailed on and the plastic positioned against them while it is lowered in a curve from that side, so as to eliminate air bubbles (fig. 11C). If the job allows of the plastic being oversize before fitting, slight discrepancies are taken care of and the edges may be trued after the sheet is fully laid.

### Windows

Clear Perspex is often used for windows, set in a rubber or plastic moulding that grips both the Perspex edge and the edge of the opening. The moulding is made to grip by forcing in a strip with a special tool, and it is almost impossible to do without this, which consists of a shaped end to fit into a handle (fig. 12A).

The Perspex panel should be smaller than the opening by the thickness of the core of the moulding, with just a little to spare (fig. 12B). Sharpness may be filed off its edges. If it is new

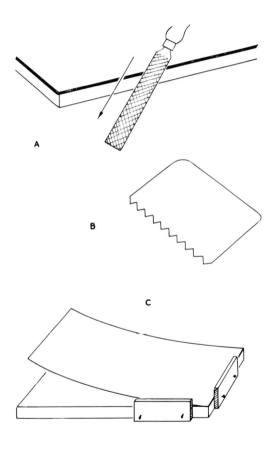

*11. File a laminated plastic edge away from the top surface (A). A metal sheet with a serrated edge will spread contact adhesive (B). Temporary guides will locate a plastic panel on a wood base (C).*

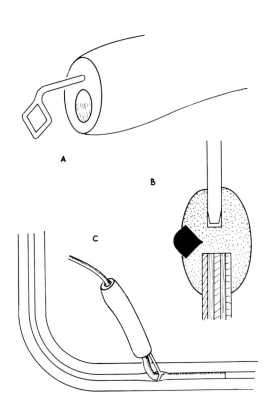

*12. Window moulding is tightened by using a special tool (A) to force in a filler piece (B) by working it along a groove (C).*

work, avoid a curve of less than about 8cm (3in) radius at a corner or elsewhere.

Press the moulding around the plywood to get its shape, but cut it about 12mm ($\frac{1}{2}$in) too long, using a knife lubricated with water. If you cut it to what appears to be the right length, it will almost certainly finish with a gap when the window has been put in. Put the moulding around the opening with the joint at the top. Spring in the Perspex panel, using soapy water applied with a slim water-colour painting brush. Rubber moulding will probably be flexible enough whatever the temperature, but some plastic moulding will be much more amenable if warm. Some fitting tools have a special end for forcing open the groove, but it can be done with the fingers or a screwdriver.

The ends of the filler piece should meet at the bottom, so start there with the tool on the piece, but the first short length will have to be pressed in with the fingers and a screwdriver. Once that is buried, press down on the shaped end of the tool around the piece, so its outline is buried in the groove and start pulling it along the groove (fig. 12C), assisted by plenty of soapy water. If you can keep going steadily, that is the best way to get an even result. If there is much resistance you will have to wobble the tool from side to side. When you get around towards the starting place, cut the filler piece a little too long and remove the tool. Press the last short length in with a screwdriver. With both moulding and the filler piece, try to get the ends butting closely together so the joints are not obvious.

| Grits | Glasspaper | Emery cloth | Uses |
|---|---|---|---|
| 50 | S2 (strong 2) | 3 | rough sanding |
| 60 | M2 (middle 2) | 2 | |
| 80 | F2 (fine 2) | $1\frac{1}{2}$ | first sanding |
| 100 | $1\frac{1}{2}$ | 1 | usual first sanding |
| 120 | 1 | F (fine) | |
| 150 | 0 | FF (double F) | |
| 180 | 00 (flour) | 0 | finest before polish |
| 220 | | | finest usual without polish |
| 400 | | | finest normally obtainable |

*Table 1. Comparative abrasive grades*

# four

# Dealing with metal

As it is a more robust material than others used in a boat, metal is less likely to need maintenance or the repair of damage, but if alterations are planned, this hardness may make the work more difficult. Care may be needed to keep metal looking attractive.

Ideally, all metals used will have a high resistance to corrosion, but this is not always so. Iron and steel rust in damp conditions, but cookers and similar things may be unprotected steel. Near-pure iron is rare today, but it had a good resistance to rust after the initial attack, as can be seen by the state of iron fittings on some old craft. 'Stainless' applied to steel is a relative term, and only that quality intended for use in a salty atmosphere should be used on a boat. Stainless steel is not as amenable to shaping nor as cheap as mild steel, so many parts will be found made of the latter.

The commonest metals on a boat are those alloys based on copper. Copper itself may be used, but it is soft and weak. Brass is an alloy of copper and zinc. The various bronzes are alloys of copper with tin and small quantities of other metals. Aluminium is increasingly used. In its purest state it has a good resistance to corrosion, but most aluminium is impure so that corrosion to the point of destruction is possible if the wrong alloy is used in a salty atmosphere. Fortunately, there are aluminium alloys which are salt water resistant and these ought to be the only choice of aluminium for a boat, even if it is only used away from the sea.

Rust on steel is well known in its red-brown form. Corroded copper and its alloys turn green, but the bronzes intended for use afloat only corrode negligibly. Corrosion on aluminium takes the form of a white powder and the surface becomes pitted. There is no treatment that will reverse corrosion. The only satisfactory course is to remove it, then apply something to protect the surface, although there are rust-inhibiting fluids obtainable from car accessory firms and there are anti-rust coats, such as 'David's Zinc 182', that can be applied to ferrous metals after loose rust has been removed, and then painted over.

## Corrosion protection

A surface protected from the atmosphere will not start to corrode, but if corrosion is present it is no use painting over it, as it will continue to spread. Corrosion should be removed mechanically with a wire brush or by rubbing with abrasive paper. If paint is to be applied, that should go on immediately, otherwise new corrosion may start.

On surfaces that are hidden or will not be touched by hands or clothing, coating with lanolin leaves a long-lasting protective film of grease; mineral oils and greases are not as effective. Steel parts should be protected by painting. Ideally, the primer should be one intended for steel, because of its longer-lasting and better grip on the surface. For parts unsuitable for paint, such as the area of a cooker near a flame, you must be prepared to clean periodically.

*Polishing*

Besides looking better, a polished surface has a better resistance to corrosion than an unpolished one. A high polish is obtainable on brass and bronze. For aluminium it is better to settle for a satin finish or merely a slight gloss. Because of its hardness, steel is difficult to bring to a high gloss by hand methods and a clean smooth surface without much shine must be accepted, preferably painted over.

The technique of metal polishing is similar to that described for plastics: breaking down the surface with successively finer abrasives until the marks from the last are so fine as to be invisible. If the effects of corrosion have to be removed, there may have to be some work with coarse abrasive. If a new edge has to be filed, it can be smoothed by draw filing with the file drawn crosswise to leave finer marks that will need less abrasive.

Wet-and-dry abrasive paper can be used, but for metal the traditional abrasive is emery, longer lasting on a cloth backing than on paper; see Table 1 for grades. After working through to the finer grades there is a choice of polishes. A liquid polish, such as Brasso, can be used on a cloth for brass, copper and bronze. For aluminium it is better to use a polish intended for silver, such as Silvo, as this will remove the slight blackening that may be left from the use of emery. Impregnated wadding (Duraglit) can be bought in brass and silver grades and may be preferred to liquid polishes, as most old soldiers will know.

An alternative to some of the emery grades for any metal except steel is steel wool–not the domestic scouring type, but that made in grades of coarseness and intended for use on paint. If a surface which was once polished has become dull and slightly corroded, metal polish may not easily break through the film of discolouration. A domestic scouring powder can be used as a means of cleaning without causing such scratches as might be made by an abrasive, then it is wiped off before polishing.

Some metal parts may have been lacquered during manufacture; this is a hard transparent film over a polished surface. Unless the lacquer has become badly chipped, it should be left. There is no way of applying such a good lacquer surface by hand. If the lacquered brass case of a barometer or similar thing has been chipped, the exposed metal may have become dull or corroded. Clean and polish these parts carefully, wipe away any greasiness, then coat with clear nail varnish, using no more brush strokes than are needed to spread the liquid.

## Shaping

If a metal part has to be shaped, light sections may be bent cold, but if they have to be softened first, different treatments will be needed. Cast or extruded brass cannot be bent, for it will break. Rolled brass in the form of sheets and strips can. Copper, brass and other copper-based alloys can be made quite soft by heating to redness and allowing to cool. After bending cold, some hardness will return, but they can be further hardened by hammering. Most cast

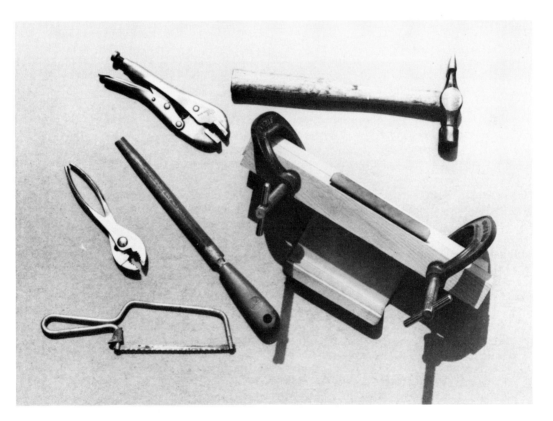

*Plate 3. Metalworking tools to take on board can include a Mole wrench, that will lock on like a vice; a general-purpose hammer, in this case a cross-pein Warrington pattern; slip-joint pliers, giving two adjustments; a half-round file; two cramps and strips of wood for sheet bending; a Junior hacksaw for all fine cutting.*

aluminium will break if an attempt is made to bend it, but strip and sheet alloy will usually bend as it is. Softening is possible by heating over a flame with soap smeared on the surface; when the soap turns black, that is hot enough. Allow to cool before bending. If strip or sheet steel will not bend cold, it must be heated to redness and bent while hot.

## Tools

There are a large number of hand and power tools for working both wood and metal. Because of the comparative softness of wood, it is possible to improvise and manage with few tools when working afloat in the confined spaces of a boat, but to do most things to metal you require the right equipment. However, there are certain tools that may have multiple uses or are more suitable for confined spaces (plate 3).

If the metal to be worked is not fixed down, a vice is needed if accurate work is to be done. This can be quite a small one with a cramp to mount it on a plank or other edge. A woodworking cramp is also worth having to hold metal to a temporary bench, pull things together and squeeze strips of wood when bending sheet metal. Mole grips are a type of lock-on pliers; they will serve as a hand vice, as well as function as pliers or a pipe wrench. A small pair of slip-joint pliers gives you two settings in the same tool. Almost any hammer can be used, but a cross-pein is more generally useful than a ball-pein.

A full-size hacksaw is needed for heavy cuts, but the lighter 'Junior' hacksaw takes up little space and will cope with many things; include some spare blades. Instead of taking on board the variety of files that could be found useful, you will find that you can do most filing with a 20cm (8in) second-cut half-round file in a good handle.

For drilling metal there is no satisfactory compromise, and you need several twist drills of the sizes required. A hand wheel brace may not be too hard work with drills up to about 4mm ($\frac{1}{8}$in plus), but above that you really need a power drill for steel. Have a centre punch to locate the start of each hole accurately.

Nuts and bolts can be quite a problem. Pliers will damage them, and a good adjustable spanner is worth having, but its end is bulky. If you want to get at a nut in an awkward place, you need a ring or open-ended spanner. That means checking what are needed and having the right ones with you. With British, American and metric sizes probable in the same boat, you may need a large collection of spanners. A good socket set is worth having, but there will be places where you still need ordinary spanners.

## Techniques

This book is not the place for comprehensive instructions on techniques, but there are a few hints that may be of use to anyone unfamiliar with metalworking on a boat. Vice jaws have teeth to grip metal, but if a polished piece is held, use sheet metal vice clamps (fig. 13A). They can be cut from a can, but would be better if made of thicker aluminium or copper which could be faced with wood or plastic for holding those materials.

Beginners often work with only a short part of a file. You get more for your effort if you hold both ends of the file and go diagonally along and across the edge, so the whole file travels the whole length (fig. 13B). To smooth an edge, hold the file firmly across it and rub it sideways (fig. 13C). Draw filing in this way removes the marks across and leaves fine parallel scratches.

Locate the position of a hole with two lines scratched across each other (fig. 14A)–any steel spike can be used as a scriber, even a sail needle–and use a centre punch to make a dent where the lines cross (fig. 14B). The centre of a twist drill does not cut. With an electric drill it is possible to force through almost any size drill bit, but if you have to use only hand power afloat, the work will be eased if you put through a small pilot hole (fig. 14C) to give clearance for the centre of the drill of the final size (fig. 14D).

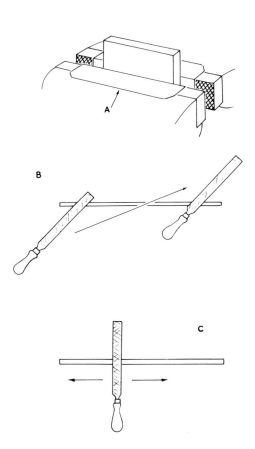

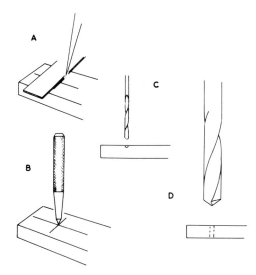

13. Sheet metal vice clamps (A) stop jaws damaging soft material. Use a file so its length is used along the work (B). Smooth the edge by draw filing (C).

14. Mark the position of a hole by scribing crossing lines (A). Use a centre punch to start the drill (B). For hand drilling it is helpful to use a small drill first (C) to provide clearance for the centre of a large drill (D).

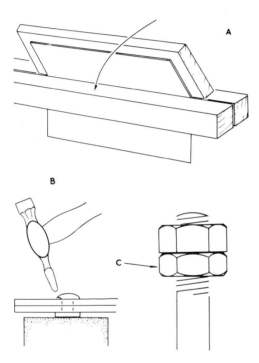

You get a better fold if sheet metal is pressed rather than hit. Grip the metal between wood or metal strips and use another piece of wood to press to shape (fig. 15A). If hitting is needed, use the hammer on the wood, not the metal.

Riveting can be done with cut-off nails as well as proper rivets. Support the head on an iron block or with another hammer. Spread the end by hammering around it with a ball-pein or a cross-pein hammer (fig. 15B) and only occasionally on top.

Lock nuts are often wrongly fitted. It is less satisfactory to put the lock nut on top of the main nut than to put it underneath (fig. 15C). Tighten both nuts down, then hold the top nut with one spanner and turn the lock nut back against it with another spanner.

15. A smooth bend in sheet metal is obtained by pushing (A) instead of hitting. A rivet can be closed by hammering around the edges of the head (B). A lock nut works best if put under the main nut (C).

# five

# Dealing with fabrics

Inside the cabin the only fabrics fairly permanently in use are curtains and upholstery. There will also be sheets and blankets or sleeping bags as well as towels. There may be carpets or mats on the cabin sole. Fabrics may be made from natural or synthetic materials. The latter have a much better and longer life in a damp atmosphere and it is unlikely that natural fibre fabrics will be found as curtains or upholstery, but many people prefer cotton to synthetic materials for sheets and pillow cases. However, as these can be taken home and laundered with household things, they do not present much of a problem.

Upholstery today is almost always padded with plastic or rubber foam, which has a good resistance to damp. Some very old upholstery may have horsehair or kapok filling, and the best treatment for that is to replace it with foam. Down or feather filling has too much tendency to absorb moisture, so should not be in boat upholstery, but if it is replaced, it is valuable stuff and should be used for home pillows or eiderdowns.

Synthetic fibres are unaffected structurally by damp. Natural fibres, such as cotton or wool, will rot. Manmade fibre fabric should not be left wet, because any dirt contained in the weave can allow mildew to form. Natural fibre will suffer from mildew before progressing to more advanced stages of rot if left wet for a long time.

It is difficult to keep pace with the types of synthetic materials used for cloth, either alone or in combination. The light types used for curtains can be washed, but heavier fabrics used for upholstery need to be dry cleaned. Another type of upholstery covering has a thin layer of plastic on a fabric backing; the fabric may be cotton but, as it is impregnated with the plastic, there should be little fear of rot.

Sleeping bags used afloat should usually be filled with polyester (Terylene or Dacron). A down-filled bag has greater warmth and a capacity for compressing more for stowing, but if it gets wet, drying is a prolonged business. Cleaning either type is a specialised process, so bags should be kept clean as long as possible and cotton or nylon liners used. If a bag is dry cleaned, it should be aired for a considerable time before use, as any fumes retained could be dangerous.

Carpets or mats should be of synthetic material with a non-porous rubber backing, so they are unaffected seriously by damp. Any other type ought to be replaced.

## Stain removal

Mild mildew may respond to brushing, otherwise put lemon juice on it and leave to dry; on heavier fabrics follow the lemon with salt. Stains caused by many things can be removed or neutralised with a commercial cleaning fluid, but check the instructions as some are liable to attack certain synthetic fibres. There are other treatments for particular stains that may be less violent.

Oil and grease should be sponged with turpentine, then rinsed and laundered or sponged with soap and water. Paint that has dried is difficult to remove without damaging the fabric. If it is still soft, turpentine will deal with an oil-based paint; an emulsion paint will respond to water. Cellulose paint will dissolve in acetone (nail varnish remover), but that will also attack most synthetic fabrics. Wash or sponge after any of these treatments.

A stain from an alcoholic liquid should be blotted immediately and rinsed with cold water; a weak solution of vinegar in water may help on heavy fabrics. Deal with tea and other beverage stains in the same way, but a weak solution of borax in hot water may follow the first blotting. Cooking fat may be removed with a solvent, such as commercial cleaning fluid. 'Polyclens' (intended for paint brush cleaning) will dissolve the fat and allow water to remove it. Otherwise a hot iron over blotting paper will melt the fat and draw it into the blotting paper.

Blood and egg can be removed if washed immediately, but may be difficult if allowed to dry; a few drops of ammonia in the washing water helps on white fabrics. On upholstery, where an excess of water is to be avoided, a thick paste of washing starch and water can be put on the stain, then left to dry so that it can be brushed off. Ink is another problem stain. For ballpoint ink, press a cloth soaked in methylated spirits (alcohol) on the stain to absorb the ink, then wash the fabric. With liquid ink, wash with synthetic detergent. Lemon juice and salt may follow to restore light colours.

Salt water or urine should be rinsed and laundered if possible; soda water dilutes the latter, and may be beneficial. If not, sponge with water and follow with a weak solution of vinegar and water.

Fruit stains may be washed out with warm soapy water, otherwise dab with methylated spirits or use commercial cleaning fluid.

Any glue that gets on fabric in a boat is likely to be a waterproof type, for which there is no treatment that will not damage the fabric; this also applies to the resins used with fibreglass. Burns and scorches are similar. The effect on the fibres cannot be reversed. A burnt appearance can be disguised by using a paste of borax and glycerine, put on and allowed to dry before brushing off.

Stains on carpets may be treated in much the same way as the heavier upholstery fabrics, but there are a few other mishaps that are probable. Rust marks, due to an iron object being left on the carpet, should be washed to remove loose powder. Oxalic acid, which is a poison obtainable from a chemist, can be used warm to remove the rust colour, then that should be washed off.

Shoe polish, potatoes and other starchy foods can only be scraped off. Grass stains may respond to methylated spirits, followed by water.

For general cleaning, curtains may be washed at the temperature recommended for the cloth, or preferably sent to the dry cleaners. Heavier woven upholstery cloth and carpets can be treated with a special shampoo provided for the purpose, but read and follow the directions;

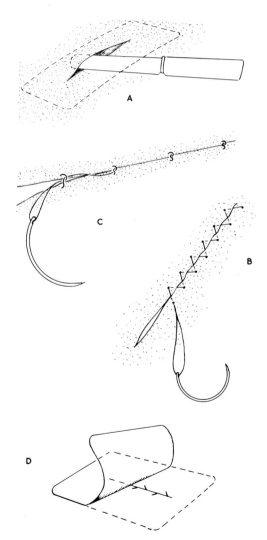

uneven use may cause shrinkage. If possible, let the material dry in a good circulation of air, by hanging it or spreading it indoors.

## Repairs

If a bunk cushion is cut or torn and the damage is slight, it may be possible to glue a patch underneath. It should be similar material and cut with rounded corners to have a small overlap all round. It may be folded to push through the damage. A table knife with a rounded end can position it and spread adhesive under the damage (fig. 16A). Latex adhesive (Copydex) will glue most open-weave fabrics.

If there is much tension on the covering, a glue-only repair may pull open and it would be stronger to stitch the edges. Simplest is a zig-zag (fig. 16B), but the diagonal lines may show on some patterns. A neater joint is a series of half-hitches (fig. 16C), with the line going along the damage between the stitches. If all of the work has to be done from one side, a small curved upholstery needle is the best tool. Carpet or upholstery thread can be bought in many colours.

Woven cloth should be satisfactory left as stitched, but the plastic-coated fabrics should have a patch over the stitches. There need only be a few zig-zag stitches, then the patch is cut with rounded corners (fig. 16D) because corners

*16. Adhesive may be put on an inside patch with a knife (A). Zig-zag stitches will pull an edge together (B), but half hitches are less obvious (C). A patch with rounded corners may be stuck on plastic fabric (D).*

left square tend to curl. The usual plastic covering is vinyl and a flexible adhesive intended for it should be used. Scrape the gloss off the surface with a knife drawn sideways just before applying the adhesive and leaving to get tacky.

*Bunk cushions*

Many bunk cushions filled with rubber or plastic foam are arranged so the filling can be removed. A common construction has piping around the seams. There is a cord enclosed in the material and with tabs extending to sew in the seam (fig. 17A). The cover is made inside-out, with the edges turned in, even if there is no piping. There may be a zip fastener at the back or one end. Even if this does not extend very far, the opening will be big enough for the foam to be compressed and withdrawn (fig. 17B). Sometimes the cover is fully sewn, but somewhere there has to be a final line of stitches made from outside. They may be over-and-over hand stitches (fig. 17C) or the edges may be pinched in a line of machine stitching (fig. 17D). If the foam is to be removed, these are the stitches to unpick. A repair can be more easily done with the foam removed, and the result should be neater.

Not every cut is in a simple position. A rip

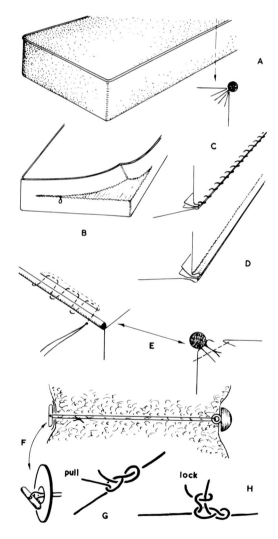

17. *A cushion seam may include piping (A). A zip fastener may allow the padding to be removed (B). The final seam will be found to be hand sewn (C) or machine sewn (D) from outside. Damage near a piped edge will have to be sewn diagonally (E). Buttons are held by knotted twine through the cushion (F, G, H).*

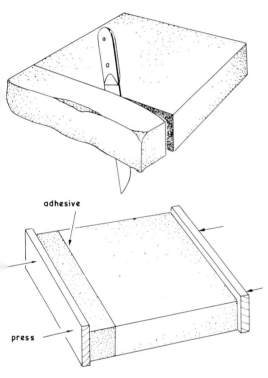

adhesive

press

*18. A damaged plastic foam edge can be cut off and a new piece stuck on and pressed tight.*

near a piped seam needs special treatment. Stitches can come close under the sound part and be taken through the far side of the damage, turned in if there is enough cloth (fig. 17E). With a curved needle it may be possible to go through the turned-under part only, so stitches do not show on top.

*Buttoning*

Buttoning is a carry-over from the days of loose fillings; the thread stopped the filling moving. Foam in slabs cannot move much, but buttoning is still used on large areas mainly for the sake of appearance, although it also stops the covering becoming baggy. If the thread or twine breaks, a new piece can be inserted with a long straight upholsterer's needle. This takes in the loop of the front button and at the back there may be a flat button or a small wood peg with a hole through. In a repair it may be necessary to put a washerlike cloth patch over the hole at the back (fig. 17F).

Compress the filling and make a figure-eight slip knot in the twine (fig. 17G). Relax the cushion and adjust the tension until the front matches other buttons, then lock the knot with a half hitch (fig. 17H). Cut off any surplus twine and work the knot into the thickness of the filling.

Latex foam fillings usually retain their shape, but some plastic foams crumble at the edges. If the cushion is symmetrical and can be turned over, this trouble can be reduced. A crumbled edge can be cut off with a sharp carving knife used wet, then another piece put on. Use a latex adhesive and press the parts together between boards (fig. 18); the joint can be covered with self-adhesive plastic strip. Position the repaired filling carefully in its cover, then the pressure when sewn in will help to hold the glued joint together.

Self-adhesive plastic strip in its many forms is useful material for repairs inside and outside a boat. The adhesive has a secure hold when pressed down, yet if it is peeled it does not leave any traces. Widths up to 15cm (6in) are made, but 5cm (2in) will deal with most repairs. Thin plastic is usual, but it is possible to get the strip with fabric embedded in the plastic for greater strength. Many colours are made, but a neutral grey can be kept for general repairs.

## Tools

Most work on boat fabrics can be dealt with by using domestic sewing equipment, but for heavier work it is useful knowing how the various needles and other items are identified.

A seaman's knife will do most cutting, but a large pair of scissors may be safer and more precise. If you have the use of pinking shears, the zig-zag edge they produce will not easily fray. If you have a sailmaker's palm for use on sail repairs, that will be valuable for pushing needles through many thicknesses of upholstery materials. Sail needles and twine will also have uses. Upholstery needles are easier to push through and coloured upholstery thread or twine will be neater.

Upholsterers' needles are described by number for their thickness and this indicates the standard wire gauge. The eyes are larger than in domestic sewing needles. Half-circular needles may have points at one end (fig. 19A) or at both ends (fig. 19B). Sizes are from 40mm ($1\frac{1}{2}$in) to 150mm (6in) around the curve. A few

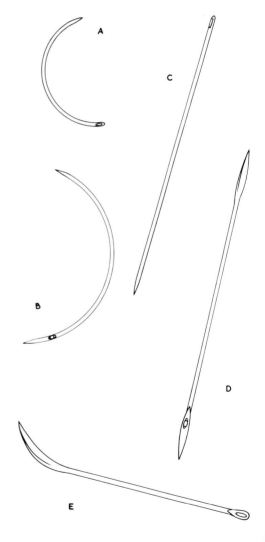

19. *Needles may be curved or straight and with plain or bayonet ends.*

single-ended 75mm (3in) should deal with cabin upholstery.

Mattress needles are the ones that go through the foam to fix buttons, so have to be longer than the thickness of your mattress or cushion. The needles can be single (fig. 19C) or double-ended and they may have broadened bayonet points (fig. 19D), which should not be needed for the usual boat upholstery.

Tool shops may have bagging needles (fig. 19E), when they have no other needles. They are straight for most of their length, but with curved bayonet points, and are really intended for sewing sacks, but one about 10cm (4in) could be used instead of a half-circular needle.

Marking out of fabric is best done with chalk. It could be a piece of blackboard chalk rubbed on a file to a chisel end, or a flat piece of tailor's chalk would be better.

# six

# Bottled gas

Bottled gas (LPG–liquid petroleum gas) is a convenient fuel and it may be used for heating, lighting and refrigeration. Used sensibly and with observation for the recommendations for installation and operation it should be safe, but there are risks in its use and this is highlighted by the fact that in America its use is strictly controlled by Coast Guard regulations. It is important that anyone performing any work on a gas installation in a boat, whether maintaining the equipment or adding more, should be aware of possible dangers and carefully observe the recommendations laid down.

Apart from the US Coastguard regulations, the British Standards Institution issues a Code of Practice. This is observed by the Ship & Boat Builders' National Federation, the Thames Conservancy Division of Thames Water and other bodies concerned with boating.

Bottled gas may be butane or propane. Butane is common in Britain, but elsewhere propane is more usual. The uses of the two gases are the same and most appliances will operate on either. Butane freezes and ceases to flow at about the freezing point of water; propane has a lower freezing point, so it will continue to flow in most temperatures likely to be experienced. In Britain propane containers are usually red, while butane containers are blue or grey. The pressure from the container has to be reduced for use, via a regulator screwed to the container. Butane and propane regulators are not interchangeable and attachments to the containers are different, but fittings further along the system may be the same. The screwed unions between the regulator and the container (bottle, tank, cylinder) have a lefthand thread (unscrew clockwise). If possible, always use a spanner supplied by the makers. Frequent use of an adjustable wrench may damage the nut.

Both gases are heavy. They are given a smell so they can be easily detected. If gas leaks in a boat, it will drop to the bilges and could cause an explosive mixture with air. If gas is suspected in the bilges, obviously avoid flames and sparks. Simple ventilation will not remove the gas. Baling with a plastic bucket is one way of removing much of it, if you do not mind being seen apparently emptying buckets of nothing over the side! Another way is to ventilate as much as possible, then blow the gas out with an air line. A vacuum cleaner set to blow might be used, but do not try to suck out the gas with it, as a spark from the motor might cause the gas drawn into the cleaner to explode.

The main points of the Code of Practice may be summarised as follows: A container should be stowed upright, equipped with a regulator and the main gas valve should be easily reached. If a container is stowed on deck, it should be protected and arranged so that any gas leaking cannot flow through a hatch or otherwise into a compartment. If below deck, the container should be stowed so gas cannot leak into an enclosed space (see below). Seamless copper piping with the minimum of joints and located as high as possible, should be used throughout, except where flexible pipes are needed at the regulator or a gimballed stove. Ventilation,

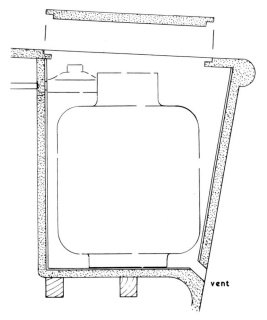

*20. A gas cylinder should have its own gastight compartment vented to the outside.*

bottom, or bigger if the container has more than 32lb (15kg) gas capacity, there should be no other openings. The code says the compartment should be made of metal of at least 20 w.g. thickness, with its joints welded, brazed or sweated with solder. Alternatively, it may be fibreglass, made with a self-quenching resin to a thickness of not less than 3mm ($\frac{1}{8}$in). Of course, there can be wood or other supports, but usually the compartment in a small cruiser will be built against the hull or transom with the overboard vent above the waterline (fig. 20). If the gas container is housed in a broad outboard well, similar safety precautions apply.

Bottled gas becomes progressively cheaper in larger containers. Anyone considering a change to a larger cylinder should remember that there must be space for it to be housed upright and it has to be in a gas-tight compartment if stowed below decks. Deposits on Calor cylinders are the same for all sizes and for butane or propane, so it is possible to change an empty of one type for a full container of another gas or size. But make sure that your system will accept the new container via an appropriate adaptor.

Containers are known by the weight of gas they hold. If a new supply is weighed, how much is left at a later stage can be checked by weighing again and deducting this figure. Because there is no easy way of checking accurately how much gas is left in a cylinder, a spare one is often carried. The same safety precautions should be observed for this as for the one in use. It may be housed on deck or in its properly lined and vented compartment; at

avoidance of draughts and insulation, as described later, are also covered. The need to only use taps, unions and other fittings intended for this type of gas should be obvious.

## Containers

The gas container should be housed in a compartment that has access at the top only and with a vent overboard through the hull of at least 12mm ($\frac{1}{2}$in) internal diameter from the all events, see that it is properly secured. If it can be arranged, it would be better to have the two cylinders in the same compartment, and the need to open the compartment and change over with a spanner can be avoided if both cylinders are connected to the system. There has to be a regulator on each cylinder and each of these connects with a short flexible hose to a T junction from which the single pipe to the system is led away. A T junction unit can be obtained on a bracket for attaching to the side of the compartment.

When two cylinders are connected in this way, only one cylinder should be turned on. If a cylinder empties, it should be turned off before turning on the other. Both should be turned off when the empty one is being removed. There are devices that will automatically change over when a cylinder empties and an indicator shows when this has happened. These can be obtained from caravan equipment suppliers (Carver Duomatic Automatic Change-over Regulator).

All flames should be extinguished when taking fuel on board. Petrol vapour can travel a long way in a boat and explode if it finds a flame. Pilot jets for a refrigerator or other appliance should be turned off and not relit until conditions are proved safe after refuelling. If separate fuel tanks are used for outboard motors, they should never be filled on the cockpit sole or anywhere inside the boat, because like bottled gas, petrol vapour is heavier than air and will find its way into the bilges if allowed: there to lie dormant until the right combination of circumstances causes it to ignite with explosive force.

## Safety

If gas leaks from a caravan installation it will usually disperse in the open countryside, so the code for caravans is not as strict as for boats; flexible hose may be merely pushed on pipes and nozzles. This should never be allowed afloat. Any replacement flexible hose should be obtained from a dealer in bottled gas equipment. Rubber and some other hoses may be attacked by the gas. There are special end fittings for flexible hose, but Jubilee and other worm-drive clips make good joints. If it is difficult to push a cold hose fully on to a pipe, it can be softened in hot water. Pipe clips are obtainable with a wing to the screw so that a screwdriver is not needed, and these can be particularly convenient for the connection to the regulator, where access is restricted.

If alterations to a gas system are contemplated, make sure that the cylinder is well away from the cooker, engine or other heat source; do not take piping through the engine compartment. Consider insulation of any appliance that produces heat, remember that heat rises. In a small cabin installation, woodwork in the vicinity of a cooker should be protected by an air gap and non-combustible material, such as asbestos. It is unsatisfactory merely to fasten asbestos directly to woodwork; there should be about 25mm (1in) between the two, if possible. Allow as much space as possible above a stove. In a large boat there might be a hood with an electrically shielded extractor, but for a small installation a mushroom ventilator may be all that can be arranged. Remember that a refrigerator running on gas produces heat, and air space around it is needed for insulation. Information provided by the makers indicates how much this should be, but complying with these limits may be impossible in a small cabin so that it may be better to settle for an icebox.

There are sometimes conflicting requirements of ventilation and freedom from draughts. When gas burns, it consumes oxygen from the air. There have been cases of people in an enclosed cabin drifting off to sleep and dying from lack of oxygen. This means that some of the cabin ventilation must be of a type that cannot be closed. There can be non-adjustable ventilation panels in doors and bulkhead–some low and some high, to encourage air circulation. Holes in the cabin sole may bring in air from the cockpit (see Chapter 1).

Draughts may affect a flame to the point where it goes out, or it may flicker and produce much less heat. Draughts on a pot will make its contents take longer to boil. Locating the cooker in relation to air circulation may have to be a compromise, and it may be necessary to use screens or erect a part bulkhead. A metal screen working in the same way as one provided for a camping stove might be put on only when cooking. It is advisable to have a cooker with failsafe devices on each burner, so the supply is cut off if the flame blows out.

*Piping*

Gas pipes for the fixed installation should be solid-drawn copper or stainless steel. The size will usually be dictated by the sizes of unions on the equipment and, in all but the largest boat, installations will be 6mm ($\frac{1}{4}$in). Routing pipes through the bilges does not comply with the code. Instead, run as high as possible and no longer than necessary, clipped rigidly. Vibration over a long period may make copper brittle. There should be clips between 10cm (4in) and 15cm (6in) each side of a joint and at not more than 60cm (2ft) intervals along a run. Corners should be taken in easy curves–not by cutting and joining.

Pipe is best cut cleanly with pipe cutters, but if an end is sawn, it should be filed squarely across and any burr removed. Joints between pipes or to appliances must be made with compression fittings. The end of the pipe has the outer screwed part and a short sleeve slid on (plate 4), then its end butts into the fitting and the external part is tightened. The effect is to squeeze the sleeve so its outside becomes curved and bevelled as it closes on the pipe. This should form a mechanically gas-tight joint, but it is usual to smear the parts before tightening with a non-setting sealing compound (Calortite) or wrap with a special tape to make doubly sure.

If a gas system is modified and any joints opened, a new sleeve should be used on a newly-cut pipe, but if an existing joint is opened and closed again, use the sealing compound liberally.

*Plate 4. Pipe joints for bottled gas are made with a screwed compression fitting, with a jointing compound to ensure complete sealing.*

During routine maintenance it is unwise to tamper with joints or unions that have not given trouble. Obviously, if looseness is suspect and tightening seems advisable, it is usually best to open the joint to add more sealing compound before drawing the parts together again. If a leak is apparent from the smell, but its source is uncertain, thick soapy water can be wiped around joints, then a leak will cause bubbles.

If the leak is slight, as it usually is, you may have to wait some time for a bubble.

For safety reasons there should be a tap in each line to an appliance. This particularly applies to stoves, heaters and refrigerators, so each can be isolated when not in use, without the whole system having to be turned off at the cylinder. It is not difficult to fit a tap, which comes with unions at each side to take the cut ends of pipe.

If an extension or alteration is to be made to the gas system, it is advisable to use new copper tubing. This is supplied soft and is easily manipulated. Bending and twisting work-hardens it, so make up your mind what you want to do to avoid too much bending and re-bending. If you want to re-use copper tubing that has been in place for some time, it may still be soft enough to reshape, but if it resists bending, do not force it as this may cause cracking or kinking. Copper tube which has become hard can be softened by heating to redness and either allowing to cool slowly or quenching in water. This can be done with a blowlamp or over a gas ring. Do not attempt softening while the tube is in position, and blow through first to make sure there is no gas inside.

Much shaping of the usual 6mm ($\frac{1}{4}$in) copper tubing can be done in the hands by pushing with the thumbs. What you have to avoid is a direct push on one place which could make the tube kink–and there is no way of removing a kink. A more even curve can be made by pulling around something like a paint can (plate 5). If the tube can be hidden after installation the

*Plate 5. A neat curve can be put in a gas pipe by pulling it around a small can.*

curve can be quite large, but if you want a neat small curve, 5cm (2in) is about the smallest radius to aim for with 6mm ($\frac{1}{4}$in) tube.

There are plastic and metal clips (some originally intended for wiring) that can be used to hold tubes in position. It seems logical to secure copper tubes with copper clips and these are easy to make. Use copper sheet about 20 gauge, and cut it with tinsnips or old scissors into strips between 5mm ($\frac{1}{4}$in) and 10mm ($\frac{3}{8}$in) wide. Hold a strip across an opened vice and use an iron rod of the same size as the tube over it. Hit this with a hammer until it is flush with

the top and the hammer has flattened the sides
(fig. 21A). Cut the clip to length, round or bevel
its corners and drill for fixing screws (fig. 21B).
If the pipe is to go into an angle, the sides can
be bent back (fig. 21C).

It is better for a length of gas piping to be
slightly too long than have to be stretched
because it is too short. The full length ensures
that end joints are pushed tight to help the
security of union at those points.

## Cookers

Bottled gas is more convenient for cooking
stoves than other possible fuels in a boat. If
used with common sense it is safe and satisfactory. There is not much to go wrong and
routine maintenance given when needed should
keep a cooker working for a long time.

A cooker burns a mixture of gas and air.
Most burners are provided with a means of
adjusting the proportions of air to gas. The gas
tap controls the supply of gas and the air
adjustment is located between that and the
burner. When the hottest flame is burning it
will be almost entirely blue with just a tendency
to white tips. This condition is obtained by
adjusting the air supply.

Air adjustment may be by a sleeve over a
slot in the pipe between the tap and the burner
(plate 6). Usually, the sleeve is sprung and it
will stay where it is put.

If the burner and pipe assembly are cast iron,
it is more likely that the adjustment is by a
machine screw which takes a spanner, but may

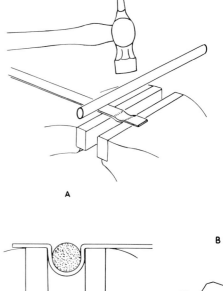

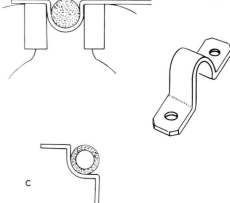

*21. Pipe clips can be made by hammering strip metal
over a vice and drilling the legs for screws.*

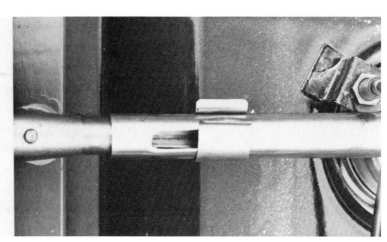

*Plate 6. On the underside of a gas hotplate there is an air adjustment for each burner with a screw action or a sleeve over a hole (as shown here).*

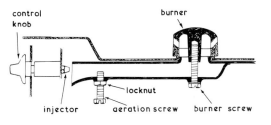

control knob
burner
locknut
injector
aeration screw
burner screw

*22. The gas/air mixture for a cooker burner has the proportions adjusted with an aeration screw or a sleeve over a hole.*

also be slotted for a screwdriver. A locknut fixes the screw when the best adjustment has been found (fig. 22). Have two spanners ready. Slacken the locknut and turn the screw. At the best position, hold the screw with its spanner while tightening the locknut with the other. Because of the play in the thread, tightening the locknut may alter the flame, so be prepared to experiment. When you have the best setting, it should not need altering again.

The gas pressure to the cooker is controlled by the regulator on the cylinder and this cannot be adjusted. If the flames lift from the holes in the burner, whatever air adjustment is made, that may be a sign that the gas pressure is too great. If the flame has yellow tips, whatever the adjustment, that is a sign that gas pressure is too low. A yellow flame makes soot and will dirty the pans, as well as give less heat. The pressure for modern cookers should be about 28 mbar (11·2 WG) for butane or 37 mbar (14·8 WG) for propane. If the correctness of pressure is in doubt, have the regulator tested by a specialist in bottled gas, or exchange it.

Behind the gas tap there is an injector directing the gas into the tube where it mixes with air. Do not interfere with the injector except that, if it is obviously partly blocked with dirt, poke this out with a fine wire–the type of pricker used with paraffin pressure stoves. Be careful not to damage the hole as a worn injector spoils the performance of the cooker.

If you have an oven, the burner for that works in the same way as for a ring, but in many makes the air/gas mixture cannot be adjusted. If you have a two-burner hotplate with a grill underneath, look for an air adjusting screw on the grill similar to that on the top burners.

Any burning device must collect some unwanted products of combustion around the holes from which the flames emerge, so dismantling and cleaning occasionally is worthwhile. Some stoves, modelled on the older household types, may have cast iron burner units that will lift away from under the top plate, but cannot be further dismantled. If they are badly corroded and choked with dirt and grease, a soak in hot water and washing soda may be the best treatment. Wear rubber gloves and thoroughly wash out any remaining soda with clean water. There may have to be some mechanical cleaning. Holes can be poked through and scraped with a knife point. A

screwdriver or other long tool may poke inside the casting and dislodge rust and dirt. Shake out anything loose and let the unit dry before reassembly.

Other stoves may have the burner unit held to the top plate with a screw from below, and the actual burner comes apart so the holes are exposed in the burner head and its collar. These are more easily cleaned by scraping each hole. Soda would be too violent in its action and any grease is best removed with soap and water. Be careful in this and other assemblies to note the sequence of dismantling, so that you reverse it when reassembling and do not leave anything out. There may be burner seals, like large washers, where the burner head closes on the top plate. Screws may have locking washers under their heads.

General cleaning of a hotplate or stove is best done while it is warm after use. Warm soapy water will remove grease and anything spilled, then the warmth will evaporate trapped moisture that may not have been wiped off. Stainless steel, chromium plate and enamelled surfaces should not need more than soapy water. Avoid soda or harsh detergents on them or gloss will be removed.

While cleaning the main parts of a cooker, give the pan support a good clean away from the stove. If there are guard rails or fiddles, take them off and clean them. Car chromium cleaner will brighten these parts and remove some of the oxidisation due to heat, even if they have lost some of their original shine. If the guard rails include adjustable bars to fit against

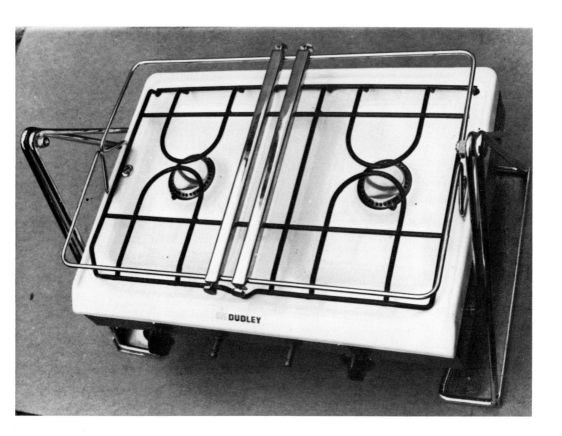

*Plate 7. A swinging hotplate may need attention at the pivot points, the burners may need dismantling and cleaning, the pan supports and fiddle should be cleaned and checked for functioning. Connections underneath, particularly any flexible tube, should be examined.*

pots (plate 7), remove the locking screws and coat them with graphite grease, so there will be no difficulty in turning them.

If it is a semi-gimballed swinging hotplate, clean and lubricate the supporting brackets. The gas connection underneath is via a short piece of flexible tubing. If this has deteriorated,

*Plate 8. If a failsafe device is provided for each burner, the positioning of its head and the security of its joints should be checked.*

it could be very dangerous. If you have any doubts about it, the cost of a short length of the correct tubing is negligible, compared with the peace of mind that goes with it. Fit the new piece in the same way as the old but, if it is a push fit, smear the metal with Calortite and use Jubilee clips around the tube.

If the stove has failsafe devices with reset buttons, do not interfere with them, except to check their security and tightness of connections (plate 8).

Check the maker's recommendations for cleaning an oven. At one time soda was usual, but with modern materials and finishes, soap and water or one of the aerosol preparations sold for household ovens are all that are needed, and anything harsher would affect surfaces.

## Gas heaters

A gas heater for the cabin is a good way to ensure warmth, but there are several points to observe if it is to be successful. Like a gas cooker it burns air from the surrounding atmosphere, but because of its size, it burns more and produces more carbon monoxide. This means that, for health reasons, a gas fire that is not of the type connected to draw air from outside should only be used in a cabin that is well-ventilated in a way that cannot be cut off or closed. In cold weather there is obviously a temptation to close all places where cold air comes in.

Catalytic heaters do not produce carbon monoxide in dangerous quantities, but other heaters without flues can. Newer ones are fitted with an atmospheric sensing device (ASD), which turns off the heater if ventilation becomes inadequate. Even if ventilation is adequate, a flame blowing out could be dangerous and many heaters are fitted with a flame failure device (FFD), similar to those advised for stoves. When a burner is lit, a button may have to be pressed and held for a few seconds, until the head of the device becomes warm enough. There is no maintenance of either device, except to see that their heads are kept in the correct relation to the flame, and free from dust, grease or soot.

A simple gas fire burns with a row of flames that play on something that glows and throws off heat. Adjustments are similar to those on a gas cooker, with a sleeve or other air adjuster, which should be moved until the flame is blue.

Any gas fire used in a boat should be fixed. The portable type sometimes used with flexible hose in caravans should not find a place in a boat, for safety reasons. If such a fire is used, it should be adapted to fix rigidly to a bulkhead or similar surface, and should be connected with copper piping.

Periodic dismantling and cleaning will improve performance. The flame plays on fireclay or metal gauze and this may become black with soot and clogged. Radiation will be better if this is shaken and scraped off. There must be a fixed guard so the hot parts cannot be touched with flesh or clothing.

A safer type of heater draws air from outside the boat and exhausts it to the outside (plate 9). Heat is then transferred through a casing to the air in the cabin, which may circulate without help, due to the fact that hot air rises and will be replaced by colder air. This may be adequate for an average cabin, or there may be a blower

*Plate 9. One type of space heater that burns air from outside and waste products are flued away, is started and controlled by knobs, without the need for an external match or other flame.*

driven electrically to direct the hot air to the cabin floor or send it elsewhere through ducts.

As most of the parts that matter are out of reach without extensive dismantling, the makers prefer owners not to attempt major servicing, which should only be rarely required. Starting is with a Piezo Igniter, operated by a push button, and it should function indefinitely. There is usually an observation window so that the spark can be seen and the lighting of the burner checked.

The air supply to the flame will be ducted through the deck or cabin top and the exhaust arranged similarly; check this thoroughly. Somewhere in the inlet pipe should be a gauze filter, which may need cleaning. There may be water traps at the low points of the pipes and they should be drained occasionally.

This type of heater is sensitive to correct observance of the starting drill. The maker's instructions will indicate what this is, but usually the gas has to be turned and pressed on, and held while the igniter button is pressed immediately, then the gas knob is held down a further 10 seconds before releasing and then used to adjust the amount of heat. If there is a thermostat, it is partly opened, then the heater started and the thermostat adjusted as required when the flame is burning. If the heater has been used and is turned off, do not attempt another start within two minutes.

If a spark appears, but the heater does not light, there may be an inadequate gas supply, possibly due to butane being affected by cold weather, a blockage or a faulty regulator. Trying a cooker or light will check the supply, except the pipe directly connected to the heater. A blocked pipe can be disconnected and blown through. A small amount of water is enough to block a pipe. Blow through with an air line or tyre pump, not by mouth, as breath contains moisture. If the heater lights and goes out after a short time, the cause is the same, although not quite as acute.

How far you go with further servicing depends on the guarantee and the maker's advice. You should have their handbook if you intend to make adjustments inside. Flame failure may be due to an inadequate supply of air, so try the heater with the inlet duct disconnected. This will show if the duct needs clearing or rearranging to give a better flow of air to the burner.

## Gas lamps

A gas lamp gives a better light than most battery electric lamps. It also produces warmth, which may be welcomed, and it does not interfere with radio or television, as fluorescent lamps may.

A gas lamp illuminates by burning an air/gas mixture against a mantle, which radiates light while most of the heat produced rises. A gas lamp should be fixed to a vertical surface, not too high or it may scorch or burn the surface above, although a deflector is usually provided above the mantle. The height may have to be a compromise in a small cabin, but space above the mantle should be at least 10cm (4in). Something can be done to protect the surface by having a metal reflector with an air gap above it. If this is polished or plated, it will also throw light downwards. A suitable reflector can be cut from chromium plated brass (photographic glazing plate) and fixed by screwing through wooden spacers (fig. 23).

The quality of light is dependent on the mantle being whole and the flame adjusted properly. Unfortunately, a mantle is a fragile object. There are long-lasting ones that are more durable at the expense of a slightly poorer light. Handle a mantle only by its base. The type that screw on are slightly better for use afloat than the type with three legs, but either will stand up to all but the roughest conditions. When a new mantle is in position, burn it off by lighting with a match and, as the flame begins to die down, turn the gas on so that it lights. In that way you should get a mantle shape that is correct and with a life as good as can be expected.

A gas lamp has a knob to control the gas supply and some form of adjustment for the air supply. In many lamps the air control is a ring which can be moved across a hole by turning it on a threaded tube (plate 10). In one version this is above the mantle, so adjustment has to be made before it gets too hot to handle. The correct mixture is easily seen by observing the varying brilliance of the mantle. Usually there is nothing but the friction of the threaded part to keep the air adjustment in place, so check that it is still correct occasionally.

Many lamps have glasses varying from simple cones to ornately decorated patterns. There is another type made from woven fireproof fibrous materials, that might be a better choice in the confined space of a small cabin where there is a risk of the lamp being hit. Cleanliness of the glass or other surround can make a surprising difference to the amount of light available, so

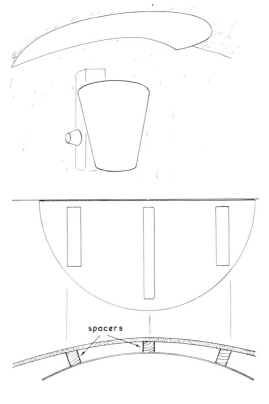

23. *A sheet metal piece held from the cabin top by packings will act as a reflector and insulate the top from excessive heat.*

removing and washing it at fairly frequent intervals is worthwhile.

*Plate 10. A gas mantle may hang by three lugs, as shown, or have a screwed connection. A spring above this one prevents it vibrating off. Air control is by a screwed collar above the heat shield. Gas control is by a knob on the side.*

## Refrigerators

In most small craft, if there is to be a refrigerator, it has to operate on gas as an adequate electrical supply is unavailable. Although small gas refrigerators are common in caravans, conditions afloat are very different and it is difficult to provide the correct conditions for proper functioning and safety. Safety considerations are such that many authorities prohibit the use of gas refrigerators in small craft, and makers may indicate that they do not recommend their products for use in boats.

The Code of Practice specifies that the burner in a gas refrigerator installed in a petrol-engined boat should be fully enclosed, and air for its combustion should be drawn and exhausted through a flame trap, or else be piped from outside the boat or from a point higher in the boat than the ports or other means of ventilation. Even then the flame should be extinguished when refuelling. All of this really adds up to the advice to anyone considering putting a refrigerator into a small cabin boat to think again and probably settle for an ice box. However, if there already is a refrigerator, the following servicing considerations apply.

A gas refrigerator only functions satisfactorily when it is upright. Moderate rolling may not matter, but if much motion is experienced the refrigerator will not work, so should be turned off. However, when the boat is stationary, the refrigerator in use should be level, otherwise the dripping refrigerant that makes it function may accumulate in pockets, and cooling will be unsatisfactory. Check with a spirit level on the ice tray shelf.

The practical use of a refrigerator in a boat

is similar to that in a house, but starting to cool is a longer process; expect at least an hour before the ice tray shows signs of freezing. Occasional defrosting is important. This is done by turning the thermostat to o, removing the ice tray and leaving the door open. Empty water from the drip collector. Put more water in the ice tray if more ice is wanted, but do not leave water there when the refrigerator is turned off and the boat left, or it may spill.

Many of the parts of small refrigerators are plastic and care is needed when cleaning. Wiping with a weak solution of bicarbonate of soda in warm water will remove dirt. Follow with a cloth moistened with clean water, then dry the surfaces. Do not use harsh cleaners. If the refrigerator has to be left, empty it of food and defrost if necessary. Empty the ice tray. Prop the door open slightly or there may be a disagreeable smell that remains for some time afterwards.

In most installations the gas burner that may need servicing is near the back and it is necessary to be able to pull the refrigerator forward to get at it. If there is a flint lighter, that can usually be attended to from the front by pulling the lighter assembly out. Note the way it goes in and see that it directs its spark correctly after replacement.

The burner may become sooted. The gas fed to it is by a small jet, which can be washed in white spirit and blown through with a foot pump. Its hole is extremely small and it should not be probed in any way. The burner should also be washed in white spirit. If any unions have to be undone to dismantle burner parts, use Calortite in the joints when reassembling. Check and clean the flue. The baffle that will be found in most installations is an important part for proper operation and should not be altered. It may be advisable to check the operation of the refrigerator while it is pulled out, by using a temporary flexible hose to the gas supply. Use soapy water around any remade joints to check for leaks.

## Other gas appliances

If a water heater is installed, it presents similar problems to a cooker and a refrigerator. If it is high, as it should be, it is less of a safety problem with its continuous flame above ventilation level and far from where escaped fumes or gas might settle. The burner arrangement is generally similar to that of a refrigerator and may be serviced in the same way. Check that flues are clear and protected. Turn off the water heater when refuelling.

There are some portable gas appliances that may have occasional use. A gas iron may be used on clothing after laundry. There can be an outlet with a nozzle to take a flexible hose. It should be mounted where it cannot be accidentally knocked. Control should be with a tap that needs more than just a turn to put it on. One type has to be pushed or pulled before turning. Because of the unsteadiness of a boat and the consequent risk of loose things moving, the outlet should not be used for a portable fire, a lead to a table lamp or anything else unsecured.

# seven

# Other domestic fuels

Although bottled gas is now the most popular fuel for lighting and heating in small craft, throughout most of the history of boating, from the earlier merchant craft to fairly recent times, lighting has been with oil lamps and cooking either with oil or solid fuel. Equipment to use these fuels is still available and may be preferred. Traditional oil lamps burned a variety of oils and some did not produce clean bright lights, but the best modern lamps, using paraffin (kerosene) under pressure and burning the vapour in mantles, offer the brightest of lights. A paraffin pressure stove can produce the hottest flames. In both cases, cost should be less than using any other fuel.

Methylated spirit (alcohol) is another liquid fuel that burns with a clean hot flame, but in Britain it is comparatively expensive. In countries where bottled gas is not permitted on a yacht, there are spirit stoves of more advanced design, comparable in many ways with gas stoves.

Solid fuel may not seem appropriate to most small cabin craft, but the experience of canal boatmen shows that quite a small enclosed heater for coal can produce comfortable winter warmth in a way that no other form of heating can.

Petrol (preferably unleaded) is used in camping stoves comparable to those used for paraffin, but because of the fire danger, these are not the stoves to have in a cabin. There are heaters that use diesel oil–in some cases as an alternative to paraffin–but most of these are intended for larger commercial craft.

## Paraffin wick heaters

The simplest way to burn paraffin is with a wick, and this form is seen in a cabin lamp, often gimballed. With this or any other paraffin burner, cleanliness is essential. It is not the paraffin which is burning that causes smells, it is excess fuel on the outside that becomes hot. It only needs quite a thin coating to give trouble, so spillage in filling should be avoided. Cleaning should be a daily task. Have the wick cut straight and the lamp glass clean. If the tank is newly filled, give the wick time to become soaked before lighting it. Charring a dry wick will necessitate cutting a new end to get a good bright flame.

Cylindrical wicks used in 'blue-flame heaters', may be in cookers or space heaters. In this case the wick fits a burner and a knob drives a rack and pinion arrangement for adjustment. This seems to reach the end of its movement while there is still useful wick left, but at that stage it must be replaced. A chimney above the flame has to be airtight; it should bed down closely and the mica window in it should not be broken. For maximum heat the burner should be adjusted to give a blue flame with just a suspicion of a white tip. If the flame is turned too high, it will smoke. If air gets under the chimney or through a broken window, the flame will not form properly.

To keep the wick level and free from carbon, a round metal trimmer is provided. Lift out the centre spreader and turn up the wick; rotate the trimmer on the wick until carbon has been removed and it is seen to be cutting all round.

*Plate 11. This remote tank for paraffin fuel has a pressure release tap on the side of the filler, a pump arranged vertically, a union for the supply pipe and a pressure gauge.*

### Pressure burners

Although the blue-flame principle is used for cookers, it is the paraffin pressure stove that produces the maximum heat for cooking. They are often called Primus, but that is the trade name of one Swedish make, and the type of cooker most likely to be found in a cabin boat is made by Taylor's Para-fin Oil and Gas Appliance Ltd.

Liquid paraffin is kept in a fuel tank, which may be away from the cooker or directly attached to it, and has to be pressurised with a pump built into it. Having a separate tank (plate 11) permits the stove to be more easily

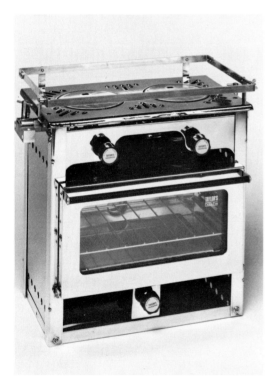

*Plate 12. A paraffin cooker has a similar appearance to a gas cooker, but starting is by preheating and maintenance includes attention to jets and other parts, as described in the text.*

jet. Slight overfilling means that the pump may have to be used frequently until some of the fuel has been used and there is a better space for compressed air. Keeping the level below the mark allows a good pressure to be built up and the flame maintained throughout a reasonable cooking or lighting period.

One advantage of a separate tank is that it can be of a larger capacity and therefore need filling less frequently. If a heater as well as a cooker is to be run on paraffin, the larger tank is worth having. It can be stowed out of the way and connected with copper pipes to both appliances, but it must be accessible for pumping. The pressure in the pipes is not very high, but joints must be soldered or made with unions that will not leak under pressure.

Paraffin, like petrol, may have a small amount of water present. The water does not mix, but settles below the oil. It is possible, although not very likely, for water to be forced through to the jet and prevent it working. If there is a fine-mesh gauze filter in the filler funnel or spout, that should stop water entering the tank. If fuel is fed by pipes from a remote tank, a water separator can be included in the line. This may be bought as a filter with a drain tap, or one can be made from copper tube about 25mm (1in) diameter; it is vertical and has its ends closed with pieces soldered on. The inlet pipe enters lower than the outlet leaves, so water that gets that far drops to the bottom (fig. 24). There could be a screw plug and washer or a tap at the bottom occasionally to drain water or anything else that accumulates there.

gimballed. Do not fill higher than indicated by the makers, as there must be some air space for the pump to provide compression. Gross over-filling will mean that the stove will not work and liquid paraffin may be forced out of the burner

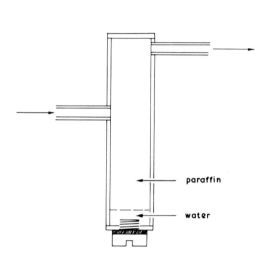

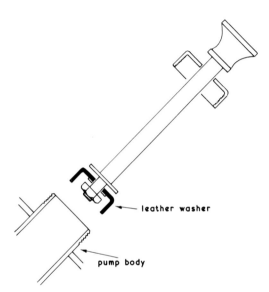

*24. A water trap can be arranged in a paraffin line, with a drain screw in the bottom of a closed tube.*

*25. Air pressure in a paraffin tank is raised by a pump with a leather washer that needs occasional soaking.*

There is a washer under the tank filler cap, which should be renewed occasionally, so have spares. If the pump meets no resistance when you operate it, its washer is dry. Unscrewing the cap on the top of the pump cylinder allows the shaft and piston to be withdrawn. Most pumps have a leather bucket washer (fig. 25). It can be soaked in machine oil or paraffin and plimmed out to shape with the fingers, then thrust into the pump cylinder again. This will revive it several times, but keep one or more spares and soak them before use.

The fuel under pressure is led to its burner through a tube and valve controlled by the knob on the front of the stove. There will be a gland where the rod from the knob controls the valve. Keep this tight or the slight leak from there may cause smell. Paraffin is vapourised by preheating, which may be done by lighting a small amount of fuel that is allowed to leak from the burner, or by burning methylated spirit in a cup or removable clip-on asbestos pad below the burner. Using paraffin for preheating causes soot, which should be removed frequently.

Methylated spirits does not form soot and may actually remove impurities around the burner. This should be the common blue type and not clear surgical spirits, which will leave the cabin with a castor oil smell. The alternative, preferable in rough conditions, is metaldehyde in tablet or jelly form.

## Burners

The burner may be 'silent' or 'roarer'. Silent is a relative term and really means less noisy; the roarer is hotter and better able to resist draughts, but the noise in a small galley is considerable. The vital part of either burner is the nipple, which is a little screw-in piece with a very small hole through it and this projects the fuel vapour. If the nipple is not perfect, cooker performance falls off. Dirt in the hole is removed by pricking with a fine wire, but too much pricking will damage it, so should not be done any more than necessary. For older stoves there are pricker wires in metal handles, and several should be kept available. Other stoves have built-in prickers.

Uneven heating or a tendency to yellow flames instead of the near invisible blue ones, indicate that the hole in the nipple is worn. Fitting a new nipple involves the use of a special tool. Pliers and ordinary spanners will not go in the confined space. For a silent burner there is a straight little box spanner; a roarer burner has a universal joint and may be tricky to use–not the repair to do while the boat is tossing at sea. A change of nipple in each burner should be regarded as a routine piece of maintenance, depending on how much use the cooker gets, but at least every year.

If the stove has a self-cleaning needle pricker, that may have to be replaced occasionally. To get at it, remove the nipple. On a Taylor stove, turn the control knob anti-clockwise so the old needle can be taken out, then turn the knob fully the other way. The needle is small and easily dropped. A magnetised screwdriver, tweezers or fine-nosed pliers will hold it. Hold the new pricker against the teeth of the spindle. Turn the knob anti-clockwise as the pricker is held close, so you hear three or four teeth click past and the needle is gripped. Turn the knob fully clockwise and replace the nipple.

If a stove is started correctly, it should give no trouble; a flare-up is usually the result of haste or a draught during preheating. To start the stove, all burners should be turned off, but without undue force. Close the air release valve on the fuel tank and see that the filler cap is tight. Pressurise the tank with the pump. A gauge may show the correct pressure but if not, the number of strokes to give is a matter of experience, but will probably be about twenty. Prime the preheating cup and light it. Wait until the preheating flame has almost burned out and turn on the control knob slightly. If a blue flame is seen from the main burner, open a little more. If the flame becomes yellow, turn off, but if it continues blue, open up and adjust to the desired heat. If the first slight turn produces a white/yellow flame, turn off and allow more preheating, then try again. If you do not achieve

*Plate 13. This paraffin space heater is for bulkhead mounting with a flue. The heating element is similar to a cooker and requires similar maintenance. The flue may have to be removed and cleaned.*

a good flame before the preheating flame dies, allow the burner to cool and start again. Cups are deep enough to provide enough heat first time in normal circumstances.

## Space heaters

Some cabin heaters use the blue-flame wick, but others are of the pressure type (plate 13), which have to be dealt with in a similar way to a cooker. The jet may not be self-pricking, so several spare prickers should be carried. These, and spare parts and tools, should be kept in a box in a known place. They may not be needed very often, but when they are, the need could be urgent.

When a paraffin heater is used, it burns oxygen from the air, so there should be good ventilation and a flue to carry away the products of combustion. A heater may be designed to throw heat forward, but some goes back and it is important to have a protective sheet (usually asbestos and supplied by the makers) behind the heater, held off so there is an air gap of 12mm ($\frac{1}{2}$in) or so between it and the bulkhead surface.

The flue can become quite hot, so there must be protection where it goes through the deck or cabin top. The fitting should suit a hole cut larger than the flue, then asbestos washers clamp over asbestos string laid around the flue to make up the thickness of the deck and keep the flue central. A polished flue will radiate heat into the cabin. Some larger types may have a water jacket, so hot water can be drawn off.

## Lights

The brightest light possible in a small boat is from a paraffin pressure lantern, often known by the trade name Tilley or sometimes Coleman, but there are other makes. Most lanterns have to be preheated with methylated spirits, but one produced by Taylor's can be preheated with its own fuel supply (plate 14).

A pressure lantern gets its bright light from a mantle, very similar to those used for gas lamps. Some mantles are of the fragile type that give the best light, but there are other more durable mantles that are acceptable. Even when the lamp is burning correctly, its glass may become slightly obscured, so routine servicing should include washing the glass.

The mechanism of the lamp is similar to a stove. The pump may need similar attention and there are washers to replace occasionally. The construction of the jet may be different from the nipple of a stove, but it is the vital part and will have to be pricked and changed occasionally.

Starting the lamp with methylated spirits may be by a clip-on pad. When this has almost burned out, the control knob is turned and the mantle should light from the remaining flame of the methylated spirits. If there is a tendency to flare, turn off and allow more heating. Adjustment of the light is by the control knob and by maintaining sufficient pressure in the tank. A thorough pump-up should give several hours light.

If the lamp uses its own paraffin for preheat, have the tank pumped, light a match and move the lever to release vapour from the automatic lighter jet. Holding the match close will ignite the vapour. Allow preheating to continue for about 30 seconds. Try turning the lantern control knob. If the mantle burns correctly, turn off the preheat lever and immediately pump up pressure in the tank to ensure a continuous light. If paraffin from the main jet tends to flare, turn off the knob and preheat more, before trying again.

It is advisable to release the pressure in paraffin tanks after flames have been turned off

and the burners allowed to cool, unless it is expected that they will be required again within a reasonable time. There can then be no risk of leakage due to poor joints or accidental turning of controls.

A test for fuel leaks can be done, whether the tank is separate from the cooker or heater or attached to it, by lighting and using the appliance under normal pressure, then turn it off and leave the system pressurised. If it holds pressure for a day, you will know the system is free of leaks.

Tanks are best filled from a can with a spout, where the paraffin does not flow until the spout is inside the tank and the level inside can be seen, so there is the minimum risk of spillage. Anything portable is best filled ashore or on deck. Filling through a funnel will produce a few drips. Cleaning may be done with something that will dissolve fuel, although a cloth damp with water and detergent may be all that is required. It is no use expecting spilled paraffin to evaporate completely in a short time. A cooker top should receive the same cleaning as a gas stove, but the burners may need removing and brushing off more frequently.

## Methylated spirit

Some small camping alcohol (methylated

*Plate 14. A paraffin pressure lamp uses a mantle. To ensure continued brilliant light, soot should be removed from the top, the glass kept clean, the pump kept in good order and the jet pricked and replaced when necessary.*

spirits) stoves are little more than cans containing something to absorb the liquid. There is no control and they are extinguished by replacing the lid; efficiency is poor. Some cookers for use afloat have absorbent tanks below the burners, but they get their fuel from a feeder tank. Burners vary, but many include a ring of jets similar to gas rings. Control cannot be very precise and may just give high and low settings. Modern methylated spirits two-burner stoves are made of stainless steel. When exposed to the air the fuel will evaporate fairly rapidly, so the covers provided should be fitted to the burners when they are out of use.

Filling should be done away from a flame and preferably outside if the tank is portable. If any alcohol is spilled, allow it time to evaporate before putting the tank or stove into its working position. If the tank has an absorbent filling, pour through a funnel slowly and continue to fill until no more can be poured in.

There are no special actions for lighting—merely remove the cover and light. In bright conditions the flame may not be very obvious, so be careful not to treat the cooker as if it were out when it is burning. The flame should burn cleanly under a pan, but if it curls around an edge, it may deposit soot there, so use broad-based pans. They will boil more quickly than narrow ones in any case.

Maintenance of a methylated spirits stove or cooker is merely a matter of general cleaning. There are no special treatments or adjustments of controls. If there are valves or taps between the feeder tank and the burners, see that they do not leak, but there is not usually any adjustment that can be made.

**Solid fuel heaters**

A small cabin stove may burn coke, small smokeless coal, anthracite or one of the other prepared solid fuels. Its efficiency depends on there being a through draught without leaks on the way. This means that maintenance should include checking its construction and any firebrick lining for cracks or loose joints, which can be filled with fireclay. The flue should have close joints, but if the stove has much use, it may be advisable to dismantle the flue, clean it through, and put it back together again after painting with a heat-resistant finish.

If a burning fire can move or be knocked over, the consequences could be serious, so check frequently that it is firmly fixed. It is also important that anything flammable is kept far enough away to be unaffected. In the original installation there should have been a metal tray fixed below the stove. There should be metal shields in front of woodwork, with air gaps between. The flue should pass through metal, with no wood or fibreglass within dangerous distance of it. A guard should be around the stove far enough away, so it does not get so hot as to be a danger in itself to anyone touching it.

# eight

# Plumbing

How much plumbing there is varies between boats. In the simplest arrangement water is kept in loose containers and toilet arrangements are 'bucket and chuck it'. Not much maintenance is required. In many craft there is a built-in water system, with hand, foot or electric pumps. There may be a chemical toilet to be removed bodily for emptying, or it may be connected to a holding tank for pumping out. There may be a marine toilet with connections through the hull. Bilge pumping has to be provided for and this can range from a bucket or a portable pump to hand or power-driven pumps permanently installed. In larger boats there may be further complications of showers and water heaters.

Some maintenance is necessary for the continued creature comfort of the crew, where failure might be annoying, but the vessel could sail on. Where there are skin fittings, however, maintenance is essential for safety. You should know where there are seacocks and other through-skin fittings and attend to them periodically. Equally important are the bilge pumping systems. Ideally there should be two, even if one is only a portable pump for emergencies.

Fortunately, most plumbing systems can be expected to run without trouble for a long time, but some maintenance will keep them running longer and it is important to know what to do and to have the right materials available if something goes wrong. Most trouble in things like pumps and other mechanical equipment used with water is due to the failure of a flexible diaphragm or valve. It is no use opening

a pump that has ceased to function, to discover the need for a piece of flexible material which you do not have. Some pump makers offer kits of replacement perishable parts, and it would be a good investment to have one of these comparatively cheap kits on board. Some makers indicate the probable life of pump parts, so replacements at around the due date may be better than waiting for the pump to let you down. If it is a bilge pump that would be important in emergency, this action will make for peace of mind.

## Pumps

A pump lifts water and then discharges it. The shorter the lift, the more efficient it should be. This means that a submersible bilge pump should work better than one which is some way above the bilges. It is also important that there are no leaks on the suction side. If there is a loose joint or a cracked pipe there, air will be sucked in and there will be a loss of efficiency, to the point where the pump will not lift water. Obviously it is desirable that there are no leaks on the discharge side, but if there are any, they will not stop the pump working. If a pump fails, or its efficiency falls off, suspect air getting into the inlet side of the system, as well as a possible fault in the pump.

The most basic pump is a plunger type (fig. 26), with an inlet valve at the bottom and another in the plunger. Small galley pumps of this type are almost entirely plastic and failure usually means replacement. Larger plunger

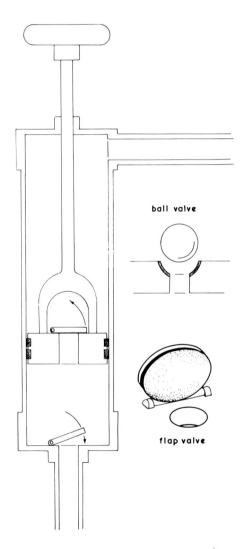

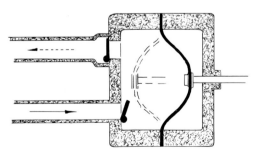

*26. A simple plunger pump has an inlet valve in the base and another in the plunger. Ball or flap valves are common.*

ball valve

flap valve

pumps (usually for bilge pumping) may have a leather washer or there may be packings around the plunger or piston. The leather must not be allowed to get dry. Traditionally it was soaked in neat's foot oil and other oils probably unobtainable now. A water pump or stern gland grease should be suitable, but do not use these on a drinking water pump.

A diaphragm pump differs in having the water always on one side of a flexible membrane (fig. *27*), which today is made of reinforced neoprene or other synthetic rubberlike material. Water is drawn in and expelled through valves. Some of these pumps have shutters over the valves, so inspection and cleaning are easy. Diaphragm pumps are increasingly used for most pumping purposes. Spare diaphragms should be kept, as well as kits of other perishables, which come with the maker's instructions.

*27. In a diaphragm pump the water is on one side and controlled by inlet and outlet valves.*

Some plunger and diaphragm pumps are double-acting, with water on both sides of the plunger or diaphragm and the valves and piping duplicated, but there are no differences in the maintenance needs.

An older type of pump popular for bilges was the semi-rotary, with its handle rocked through about 90 degrees, alternately opening clapper valves in a rocker for inlet and outlet. The better types were all-brass or bronze and should need no maintenance, other than clearing debris that jams a valve open; many however have cast iron bodies with yellow metal for the rockers. If one of these is left unused for a long period, it could rust up. It should be opened occasionally and dried, then the iron surfaces coated with water pump grease.

Gear-type pumps work well if submerged, or nearly so. As there are no valves, there is no maintenance except lubrication of the moving parts.

All other pumps rely on valves, which cease to function if choked with something that prevents their closing. It is therefore important to allow ample entry for water, while solid things are stopped. There should be no trouble with those in a drinking water system, but the intake of a bilge pump should be via a strum box or filter. This may be a sort of cage of wire gauze (fig. 28A), or a length of lead pipe could

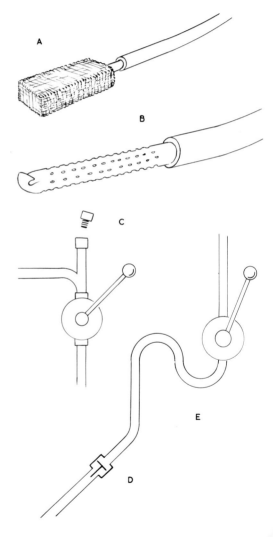

28. *A filter in the bilges may be gauze (A) or a perforated pipe (B). There may be provision for priming (C), or water can be held in the pump by a non-return valve (D) or a double bend in the pipe (E).*

have its end hammered closed and a large number of holes drilled along its length (fig. 28B). As the holes or gauze must pass enough water, even when partly blocked with debris, the filter should be reasonably large and kept low so as not to go above the water until only a negligible amount is left. The filter should be accessible for cleaning, particularly as something like a sheet of polythene could block it completely.

Electric pumps must rotate at high speed, because that is the way an electric motor operates. Consequently they are of the gearlike impeller type. Choking is unlikely, but the plate and packing over the impeller should be removed occasionally to check the need for cleaning. The makers will indicate if lubrication is needed, but in general oil and electric motors do not go well together and they are sealed so that no more oil can be introduced.

A modern pump in good order should lift water any of the heights within a boat without the need for priming (filling with water from above). A few quick strokes should draw the water up from dry. If this does not happen, the fault is probably in one or more valves. Flap-type valves should bed down tightly and may be prevented from doing so by a matchstick or something much smaller, but in an older pump there may be pitting of the metal or deterioration of the facing material. If there is sufficient thickness of metal to allow it, the surface may be smoothed with emery cloth around something flat. If the trouble is with leather or neoprene, replace these parts.

Sometimes a pump has a means of priming provided. Older plunger pumps were often open at the top for discharge over the deck and for preliminary priming. Another type may have a section of pipe above the pump where water can be poured in (fig. 28C). A non-return valve could be included in the intake pipe (fig. 28D), so there should always be water in the pump. Another way of ensuring this is to include an S-bend in the pipe, to above the pump level (fig. 28E).

*Glands*
Some pumps and other items rely on glands around moving parts to prevent leakage. A slight leak may not matter on a bilge or galley pump, except that it is a nuisance, but on other equipment, such as on the discharge side of a toilet, gland tightness is important. In the usual gland there is a packing around the shaft (fig. 29A) and a nut that can be tightened to compress it.

Normally a slight leak can be cured by tightening the nut, but a point will be reached where no further tightening is possible and it is necessary to renew the packing. This packing may be like string, impregnated with a water-resistant lubricant. Traditionally this was tallow. The smallest sizes are 2mm or 3mm diameter ($\frac{1}{8}$in or less) round section, but larger sizes are more likely to be square. It is better to renew packing completely than to put new on top of old. Make sure all particles of the old material are removed and the space is clean. Move the shaft up and down or rotate it, to

check for grit or other matter that might interfere with a watertight joint.

The small round packing is merely wound
around until there is enough, but there can be
several pieces to make up the thickness. That
is how packings are put into domestic water
taps. With the larger square section packings it
is better to cut them into separate pieces so they
bed down better, without the uneven ends that
come from spiralling around. The best way is
to cut the packing in the same way as is usually
done for stuffing boxes in stern glands. Wrap
the strip around a rod of the same diameter as
the shaft and slice diagonally (fig. 30). Position
the pieces in the gland so the joints are
staggered.

Some more recent glands will be found to
have synthetic O rings as the water-barrier
(fig. 29B) instead of packing material. If
tightening does not cure a leak, a new ring will
have to be fitted.

In an old piece of equipment there may be
leaks at one end of the stroke only, and this
indicates a worn shaft. Stopping that sort of
leak completely can only be by replacing the
shaft as well as the packing. In emergency a
piece of light line soaked in water pump grease
can be put on top of the old packing and
tightened down, but this is unlikely to be
effective for long and the whole packing should
be replaced later.

## Piping

With the coming of plastics, much water piping

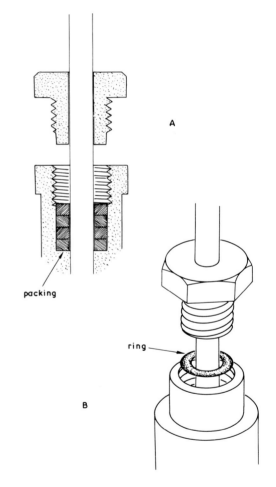

29. *A pump gland may be kept watertight with a
packing (A), although some have a compression
ring (B).*

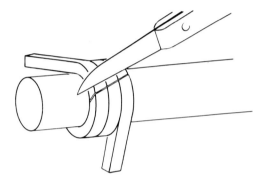

*30. Square gland packing material is best cut into
rings for a close fit.*

in a boat can be made from plastic hose, simplifying the work of installation or alteration. However, most of the plastics used are unsuitable for hot water, as they will soften. These are the common PVC and polythene, but nylon hose has a better resistance to heat. Sizes available are from 6mm to 50mm ($\frac{1}{4}$in to 2in). Many pieces of equipment for use in water systems have spigots to take plastic hose, which can be softened with hot water and pushed on. There should be no need for pipe clips as the hose will shrink tight as it cools, but they could be used in the same way as described for gas hose.

Ordinary plastic hose may not be strong enough for the suction side of a pump, as its wall may cave in; for this use there are corrugated hoses. Some are spiral-wound with metal included for strength.

If a plastic hose has to be attached to a

fitting that is screwed to take metal pipe, it may be possible to fit a short length of metal pipe in the joint and attach the plastic hose to that. For the smaller plastic hoses there can be metal ends. A garage may have the equipment to insert a spigot and secure it by crimping a ferrule around it.

Steel pipes have been used for water systems afloat as well as ashore, but they should be galvanised. Some fittings are screwed to take standard steel pipes. Threads are to B.S.P. (British standard pipe) specification, but they are changing to metric. If an alteration has to be made and suitable screwing tackle is unavailable, the pipes may be taken to a household plumber to cut the threads. Pipes are tightened with a pipe wrench, which is a sort of adjustable spanner with teeth. Screwed joints should be sealed, either with a jointing compound smeared on the threads or by binding with PTFE tape, which looks like plastic electricians' tape.

Copper tubes are suitable for drinking water systems. The hard straight tubes used for household central heating systems may be used, but soft copper tubes of the same sizes but supplied in coils, are more suitable for alterations and the curves of a boat, as they are easier to work. Most used will be 12mm and 18mm sizes ($\frac{1}{2}$in and $\frac{3}{4}$in). There are stainless steel tubes available for similar uses. Much bending of copper tubes can be by hand or around improvised formers, but there are bending jigs obtainable from tool hire stores.

There are compression fittings for copper pipe ends, similar in principle to those described for gas pipe joints, and they may be needed to join to certain equipment. Elsewhere good joints can be made by soldering. An outer fitting has solder already in a groove. The meeting surfaces are scoured clean, usually with steel wool or emery cloth, just before coating with flux and putting together. The lead/tin soft solder does not require much heat to melt it. A flame from a gas blowlamp is played on the joint until a silvery line shows at the edge of the joint to indicate that the solder has melted.

Plastic tubing is fairly stiff, particularly when cold. If more flexibility is needed, rubber or neoprene hose can be used and there are canvas-covered rubber hoses for use where strength is required. Rubber is affected by sunlight, so will last longer if kept shaded.

Clear or semi-clear plastic may seem more hygienic than coloured plastic, but it lets light through and this causes algae to form. Although this may be harmless, it looks unpleasant, particularly in a drinking water supply. Hoses and jerrycans and other water containers would be better coloured. Blue seems to be the best preventative colour. If algae has occurred, it may be removed from clear plastic with a solution of a denture cleaning fluid, which is allowed to swill backwards and forwards before being washed out; a weak solution of household bleach may also be effective; formalin solution can also be tried. In all cases, a thorough washing out with clean water should follow. If there is a bad attack, the only solution is a new length of pipe. Do not use carbolic or other strong disinfectants in a drinking water system.

## Tanks

Older water tanks may be galvanised steel. The zinc coating is not of indefinite life and there may be rust inside. There should be an inspection cover large enough to shine a flashlight into an empty tank and see its condition. Special protective paints for the insides of water tanks are available, but these are intended for large tanks in ships. Applying them successfully through a small inspection hole may be impossible and a rusted tank may have to be scrapped. It might continue without leaking for a long time and the water from it only used for washing, while drinking water is drawn from other containers.

In many fibreglass craft the water tanks are moulded in and are made entirely of fibreglass, often with no inspection cover, so nothing can be done to their insides. These and galvanised steel tanks could be washed through with the liquids recommended for cleaning plastic hoses; if the water tastes of styrene, try washing the tank with a strong mixture of vinegar and water. Flexible water tanks do not normally need any special treatment, except washing out with clean water. At longer intervals a tank may be filled with fresh water, to which has been added a cupful of non-biological household detergent powder. Leave this for a few hours, then wash out with several changes of water.

## Sinks

Galley sink outlets need more frequent atten-

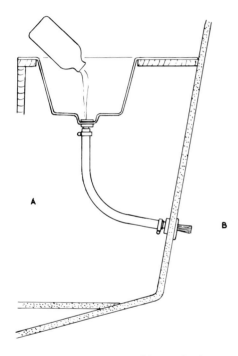

replace it with a new one, but scrape and scour dirt from the metal or plastic ends while they are accessible.

If the pipe is metal and you do not wish to remove it for cleaning, plug the skin fitting and pour in one of the domestic cleaners advertised to 'kill all known germs' (fig. 31B); more than one treatment may be needed. Use a domestic cleaning powder on a stainless steel sink, but do not use it so heavily on any plastic insert for the outlet. However, if you are in the habit of emptying the contents of the teapot into the sink, there will be tannin stains to scour off.

We tend to use water sparingly afloat, because of the limited supply, but water from around you is plentiful and there is much to be said for having a salt water tap at the galley sink. For one thing, a wash through the outlet from the sink with a plentiful supply of salt water, or even water from a river, when the boat is to be left between week-ends, should move on those things that might be producing a foul smell by next week.

If there is already a water inlet for an inboard engine, it may be possible to tap off that, with a T fitting, and lead a plastic hose to a hand pump at the sink. However, make sure it is marked prominently, so a guest will not draw from it for cooking. Alternatively, there can be another underwater inlet for this supply, but if you do not want to make a hole through the hull, it may be possible to have a length of flexible hose to drop over the side when needed.

In most small craft the water system is not under pressure and water is drawn by hand,

*31. A sink outlet may be cleaned by pouring in disinfectant while the skin fitting is plugged.*

tion than they often get. A household sink outlet has a double bend to trap water and prevent smells. Many galley outlets go direct to a through-hull fitting and they can get foul inside, so unpleasant smells return. If the skin fitting is above the waterline, the pipe may be satisfactory as a piece of plastic hose, with clips each end (fig. 31A). As plastic hose is cheap, the best treatment for a foul pipe is to foot or electric pump. There are a minimum of things to go wrong. In another unpressurised system, the action of turning on a tap causes an electric pump to cut in. In a pressurised system, the tank has to be filled with a hose having screwed connections so that mains pressure forces the water in and flow at the taps is caused by air pressure in the tank, built up by an electric compressor.

If a major fault develops there will have to be a replacement part, but in any of these systems that rely on a pump, routine servicing should include checking joints, so air cannot enter pipes or escape from a pressurised tank. If an electric pump is involved, look at the electrical connections. Most pumps were originally intended for caravans and the brass used in connections may corrode rapidly in a salty atmosphere. Open a doubtful terminal and scrape the contacts clean before coating with Vaseline.

The filler for a pressurised system will be above a non-return valve, but the cover provides further protection. Renew the cover washer occasionally.

If a shower is provided, the maintenance of its piping and outlet is the same as already described. The shower head actually passes a much smaller amount of water than the one at home, reflecting the limited quantity available. If you use much hot water, the inside of the shower head may become furred with lime. This has to be removed mechanically or it further restricts the flow. Usually a screw at the centre of the shower head allows the rose to be removed, and it may be in sections so you can scrape half holes or poke through others, taking care not to enlarge them.

The pipes of a water heater may suffer in a similar way, normally only on the delivery side of the heating flame or element. If hot water is delivered via a spray over the sink, this will need cleaning occasionally like the shower. If the delivery pipe joint is opened, the build-up of lime can be checked. It can probably be poked out of a short pipe, but in a bad case the pipe may have to be replaced.

## Toilets

In recent years policy regarding toilets or heads afloat has changed. It is now illegal in Britain to use a toilet that discharges through the hull on all inland waters, as it has been in the U.S.A. for a long time. This also applies to many harbours, marinas and similar places on tidal waters. Consequently, many toilets are self-contained chemical ones, or are connected to holding tanks for pumping out, and fewer boats are equipped with direct discharge marine types.

With modern chemicals making the contents odour-free, self-contained toilets that have to be taken ashore for emptying are acceptable. It is advisable to use the fluid recommended by the makers and in the correct proportion, otherwise fumes can cause a slight irritation to the nose. Have a measure, if the container is not marked. It is inadvisable to leave a partly-filled chemical toilet for long periods unused as smells or marking of the plastic container could develop. Empty and recharge if the boat is to be left for a period of weeks.

If there is a flushing water hand pump, parts for this and spare filler and discharge covers might be kept as spares.

If the toilet flushes into a holding tank, which is then pumped out, follow the maker's instructions regarding chemicals, which break up solids as well as disinfect and kill smells. There may be an electric macerator in the line to break up solids. Except for checking corrosion of electrical connections, this should not need attention. If your installation depends on a suction pump ashore to empty the holding tank, routine maintenance consists of checking security of fastenings of the toilet, tank and other equipment, with a look at pipe unions and the pump-out connections on deck. If you have your own pump for alternative discharge through the hull at sea, check the two-way cock, particularly if it has been a long time without use. See that it works both ways without leaking when there is liquid in the system, but if it has to be opened for adjustment or repacking a gland, do that immediately after a pump-out.

The usual shore pump out is normally efficient, but occasionally it helps to flush through a considerable amount of fresh water to remove anything lodged. Ideally, pump and flush out normally, then introduce clean water with a hose into the toilet until the holding tank is full. If possible, rock the boat while doing this, then pump the tank dry, to ensure its inside is as clean as it can be made.

With a marine toilet there are two main considerations: the works of the device itself and the through-hull connections. There are a large number of different makes of marine toilets, but the best-known in Britain are the products of Blake and Simpson-Lawrence. Designs of these change, but the basic Blake toilet has a soil pump and another to remove the contents of the bowl. The Simpson-Lawrence toilets have a double-acting pump dealing with both actions. These have normal seats and covers, but a Lavac toilet has an airtight cover so, when the single discharge pump is used, the vacuum created in the pan draws in the flushing water.

Continued satisfactory use of a marine toilet depends on the observation of a few rules. If it is not abused, and routine maintenance is given when needed, it should have a long life. Make sure everyone on board understands operation of the WC, particularly what can and cannot be done. Nothing must go through the toilet that it is not intended to take. Cigarette butts, matches and other solid things that a person may be in the habit of dropping into the pan at home may prevent operation or cause leaks. Do not use soft toilet paper as it disintegrates into fibrous pieces that may jam working parts. Do not pour through oil or petrol, as these will attack rubber parts.

There is ample water available, so flushing should be thorough. This will reduce smells and reduce risk of the pan staining. Domestic toilet cleaning fluids are unsuitable as they may damage internal parts. Blakes say you can use a little diluted Jeyes Fluid; soapy water can also be flushed through. They discourage the use of cleaning powders when the toilet is in the boat. If the pan becomes stained, cleaning with scouring powders should only be done when the toilet has been removed from the boat and dismantled.

If pump pistons need lubricating, soft soap should be used, not oil or grease, although that may be needed in some glands. External linkage may be oiled carefully, but avoid an excess that might mark clothing. Display the maker's instruction card prominently and maybe add your own instructions, so visitors can learn what to do, to avoid embarrassment and possible damage to the toilet.

The pump spindles pass through glands or stuffing boxes and these may be tightened if leaks develop or repacked during more detailed servicing, as already described.

Because of the confined space in which most toilets are located, major servicing is best done away from the boat. This involves disconnecting hoses and undoing the hold-down bolts (plate 15) so the unit can be lifted away. The toilet away from the boat may not seem such a mysterious machine, but if you do not want to dismantle it yourself, the makers and some yards offer reconditioning services.

### Toilet pumps

The pumps and valves are the parts most likely to need attention. Some piston-type pumps can be opened from the top and the plunger withdrawn. If not, the pump has to be unbolted and

*Plate 15. If a marine toilet is removed from the boat, the condition of its pump, glands, screwed fastenings and the movement of parts can be checked, as well as all of the assembly thoroughly cleaned.*

lifted from its base so that the plunger can be dropped. Tightness of fit in the pump cylinder may be assured by one or more synthetic rubber rings sprung into grooves in the plunger; new ones are easily fitted. Blake plungers include a valve, which is a ball on a seating, and a similar arrangement may be used for the inlet valve; in both cases the ball and its seating may have to be replaced. Flap, clapper or clack valves are, however, more usual. Suction causes the hinged door to open and compression shuts it, so that water tightness depends on a rubber or plastic weighted flap or washer. Although these can be bought, some can be cut from plumbers' 'insertion' sheet material. There are other places where gaskets come in joints to make them watertight. The makers can supply new ones, although it is possible to cut your own, but watch that different thicknesses do not affect the lining up of parts. Jointing compound can be smeared on the gaskets.

Makers provide exploded views of their toilets with lists of part numbers (fig. 32). Get their drawing before dismantling, as this provides a guide to the sequence of work where it is not obvious, and you will know what parts you have to order or fabricate yourself. Maintenance is more satisfactorily done when there is no rush to get the toilet re-installed again. Allow time to clean all parts, and give the metalwork a coat of paint, so the toilet goes back looking hygienic and efficient. Paint the boat where it is to be fitted, while the surfaces are accessible.

Makers know what parts are likely to need replacing during overhaul and you should check what kits of spares are available. Many of the flexible and perishable parts are intended for once-only application and it is inadvisable to remove the many washers and packings with the intention of using them again, when replacements are quite cheap, and their use will give you confidence in the functioning of the toilet for another period. The makers may offer special tools, but it should be possible to dismantle and re-assemble using tools from the usual amateur mechanic's kit.

## Skin fittings

There are several skin fittings and sea-cocks that may be used at various points through the hull and, while it is those for the toilet that may be expected to need most attention, don't forget the cockpit drains, which are usually out of sight and thus easy to overlook during routine servicing. Faults in them could sink the boat, so their maintenance is important. When the toilet is removed for maintenance, the sea-cocks should be attended to while they are easy to get at. Skin fittings without cocks should only be installed above the waterline, but their method of mounting should conform to the same standards as below-water sea-cocks.

Securing bolts should pass through a reinforced part of the hull. In some fibreglass hulls the sea-cock may be moulded in. Check around it for signs of cracking, indicating moving or loosening. A fibreglass skin should have a wood pad with the hole through. Where a sea-cock is bolted down, check the bolts for tightness, and look at the flange outside for proper bedding down. If the bolts are not known to be fully seawater resistant, withdraw one or more to look for corrosion. Like keel bolts, corrosion

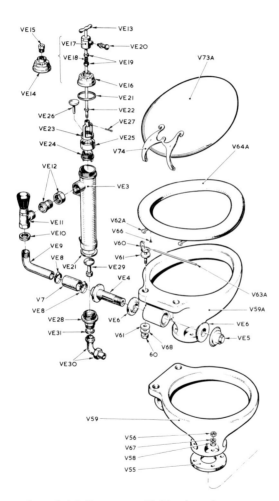
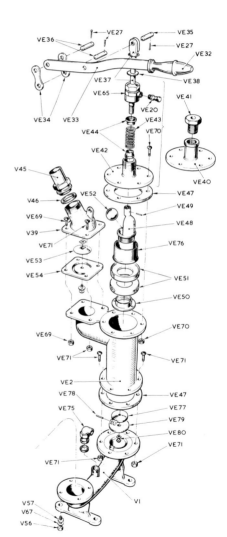

*32. An exploded diagram, provided by the makers, shows how the parts are assembled and gives the reference numbers if replacements are needed. This is a Blake 'Victory'.*

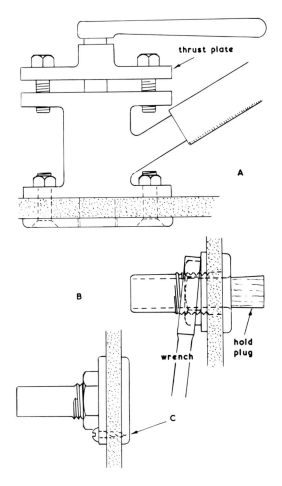

thrust plate

A

B

wrench

hold
plug

C

*33. Tightness of a valve in a seacock may be controlled by a thrust plate (A). A plastic skin fitting may be held by a plug, while the nut is tightened (B). This can be prevented from loosening with a screw (C).*

and thinning to weakening point is liable to happen out of sight in the thickness of the hull.

If the sea-cock has a screw-down, or wheel valve, its function is similar to that of a stop tap in a domestic water supply. The gland may need tightening occasionally, but only rarely will the sea-cock have to be dismantled. Another type has a metal-to-metal ground-in tapered plug to ensure watertightness, and there is a thrust ring or plate which can be adjusted above the cone; the sea-cock is turned on and off with a handle that rotates the plug. Adjustment of the thrust plate has to be arranged so it gets the valve tight, while still allowing freedom to turn the handle (fig. 33A and plate 18). If there is still leakage when the thrust plate has been tightened, the metal surfaces may have become pitted with corrosion or have become scored with trapped grit. It may be possible to improve the fit with grinding paste between the surfaces, which are moved in relation to each other. Make sure all paste is wiped off before final assembly.

The hose connection to the toilet may be of plastic, but choose the semi-rigid reinforced type recommended by the makers and secure the ends with clips.

Plastic skin fittings, as used above water, are immune to corrosion problems. The usual type relies on one large nut inside. If one of these fittings is loose, unscrew it and coat all meeting surfaces with jointing compound. If the inner part is difficult to hold, push a tapered piece of wood into the hole to grip while tightening the nut inside (fig. 33B). A woodscrew driven from inside through the flange of the nut will prevent later loosening (fig. 33C).

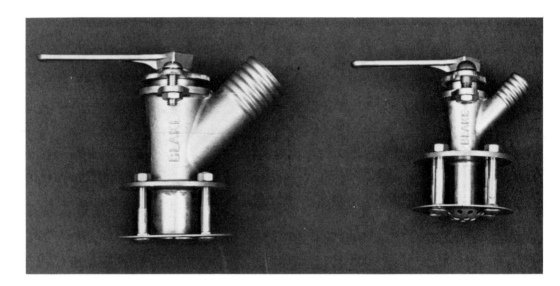

*Fig. 16. Skin fittings and seacocks for a marine toilet have screws through the skin, which should be checked for condition and tightness. Screws through the pressure plate may need tightening. Action should be checked by moving the handles. Hose connections should be clean and tight. If there is an inlet filter, it may have to be cleaned or replaced.*

## Bilges

Modern boats should not leak through the hull and the only bilge water may come from rain or spray, but the old tale that some water in the bilges is a good thing was probably never true and certainly does not apply today. Bilge pumps should remove water only, but it is difficult to avoid small pieces of rubbish finding their way into the bottom and there should be a periodic inspection and cleaning of the bilges. Deliberately putting in water and pumping it out may wash debris to the lowest points, but there may be still some elsewhere to remove. As well as that, ventilation of the bilges is never as good as it should be, so if the ship is to be sweet, cleaning out of caked-on dirt and grease is worthwhile, even if not the most attractive duty.

Warm water and detergent, with a cloth and scrubbing brush, may be all that are needed. Start at the higher parts of the bilge and mop out from lower down. A portable bilge pump may have its uses. If the hull has frames, look for dirt lodged behind them and blocked limber holes that will restrict the flow of bilge water.

There are special cleaners that disinfect as well as clean. Some of them, such as Sail 3 Bilge Clean can be used in salt water as well as fresh, so if you are cleaning away from a precious fresh water supply, one of these is worth having.

What to do to the bilge depends on the boat. If it is fibreglass it could be left as it is after cleaning, although it could be given a coat of paint if you wish. A wooden hull should be painted. This may be similar paint to that used elsewhere on the hull, but some manufacturers offer special bilge paints. Traditionally the bilges were given a coat of black varnish–a tar-like product. This is also a good finish for any iron ballast in the bottom of the boat. Lead ballast does not need paint.

Clearing out equipment, lifting bottom boards and cleaning the bilges can be a dirty job that will mark other parts, so it is advisable to deal with the bilges before tackling general cleaning of other parts higher in the boat.

## Winterising

Like plumbing systems ashore, precautions must be taken if the water temperature is expected to go below freezing, as the ice which is formed takes up more space than the water which produced it, so whatever surrounds the ice may burst. Fortunately, plastic pipes may expand enough to take care of the greater volume, but some plastics which are normally flexible and soft become hard and brittle at low temperatures so that their capacity for expansion should not be relied on. There are other more rigid materials which would be damaged by the water freezing, so the system should be drained when the boat has to be left and there is a possibility of frost.

It may be possible to include a drain tap in the system, but because of the need for some piping to conform to the shape of the hull, doing this at the lowest point is not usually practicable. It may be simpler to disconnect a joint at a low point and let water drain from there. Because of the loops and bends in piping, not all water will run out and the only way to remove it is to blow it out from another released joint. This might be done by mouth in a small boat, but if the piping is very long there will have to be pressure from an air line or pump.

More of a problem than the piping may be some of the components which trap water. To get the water out of most pumps, disconnect the inlet hose and use a piece of wire or your finger to push the inlet valve open and release the trapped water. When dealing with a gear type or other rotary, or semi-rotary pump, the cover plate will have to be slackened or removed so that the water will drain away. If any pump is installed at an angle so that water will not drain by gravity, a syringe may be needed to draw out the last of the water. Operating a pump while draining will help to force water out and its feel or sound will show when it is clear. However, do this gently by hand as some power pumps will suffer if run fast when dry.

If there is a double bend under a sink, it may be possible to blow water through, or it can be sucked out with a syringe.

A marine toilet needs special treatment if it is to remain in a boat during a time of frost. Close inlet and outlet sea-cocks. Disconnect the inlet pipe from the sea-cock and flushing pump, use a wire or your finger to release the inlet valve and hold it open until all the water has drained out. Disconnect the discharge pipe at the sea-cock and put it into a bucket or other container and pump out the discharge water. Mop out the bowl. Put a notice on the toilet, and tie down the lid to remind yourself as well as others that the appliance is inoperative.

Obviously, a drinking water system cannot be prevented from freezing by adding an anti-freeze solution, such as is used in cars, because of the near impossibility of removing it afterwards. Ice on bilge water may not matter, but it would be better to dry the inside of the hull. Salt water has a lower freezing point than fresh water, so if freedom from water in the bilges cannot be relied on, salt in the bilges will help to prevent freezing, and will do no harm to a wood or fibreglass hull.

# nine

# Electrical work

Electrical equipment and systems on a boat may be more troublesome than other things and need more care and attention, mainly because damp and electricity do not go together. There is a tendency to use electricity more on modern boats than was once the case. Not only are electric lamps used where gas and oil lamps were once normal, but there are more instruments and other electrically-powered equipment which add to convenience, safety and efficiency. This means that all parts of the electrical systems of a boat should be maintained in first-class order.

Power comes from a battery, which is an assembly of cells to make up the required voltage. Because of the problems of sheer bulk, the voltage has to be kept as low as is acceptable for the boat's needs. In the smallest boat, with minimal electrical equipment, it may be possible to manage with a 6-volt battery, but it is more usual to have a 12-volt system similar to that found in most cars. Larger craft will use 24 volts, but it is unusual to have anything bigger than this. This has to be compared with the 220 volts of the British domestic system, or the 110 volts of the American supply. The difference is considerable and the much lower voltage cannot cope with faults and resistances in the system in the way that the higher voltage might.

Put non-technically, voltage is the pressure which pushes the electricity around, while ampères are the measure of what is being pushed. Watts are the units of power and are merely the product of voltage and ampèrage, so 12 volts multiplied by 5 ampères gives a power of 60 watts. If the battery is only 6 volts there would have to be 10 ampères to give the same wattage, while 24 volts would get the same results with 2·5 ampères. Ohms are the measure of the resistance of the conductor through which the electricity is passing. Obviously, it is an advantage to keep the resistance to a minimum. Because resistance gets less as the cross-section of the conductor gets more, it helps to use wires as thick as possible. It also helps to keep the wires short, as a long wire has more resistance than a shorter piece of the same section. Or put the other way: if you must have a long wire, it is better thicker than thin. There will always be some voltage drop over wires of great length and this must be allowed for, but in the size boat most of us have, wire lengths should not be enough to cause trouble.

## Wiring

For most boat wiring it is better to compare the needs with those of a car rather than a house. Car wiring suits the low voltage of a battery and much of the system is similar to that of a boat. The sizes of wires for car work are mostly suitable for boats, but if there is any doubt, go up a size. At one time rubber was the usual insulation, but it gets porous as it ages and damp may penetrate these pores, causing leakage. Some boat wiring was encased in metal tubes. Old wiring with rubber insulation or metal casing should be regarded with suspicion. Besides porosity admitting water and causing leaks, rubber may be attacked by oil, so such wiring in the vicinity of the engine may suffer. Modern wiring has plastic insulation, which does not deteriorate so badly with age and is unaffected by oil. Any alterations to a boat's wiring should be done with plastic-insulated wires. In most situations it is sufficient to fix the insulated wires at frequent intervals with clips (fig. 34A), but if protection is thought advisable, there are plastic conduits available; these will serve as well as metal ones, without the risk of shorting.

Use copper wire, as it is the only metal with good conductivity for low voltages. Smaller wires are single, but others may be made up of three or seven strands twisted together. This gives some flexibility for bending into place, but do not confuse these with 'flex' such as is used for plugging lamps and fires into household mains sockets. In general, flex should be avoided afloat, except for short lengths to fittings where some movement is necessary. Table 2 gives the current rating of some types of cable.

Cables for boat wiring may be single or twin core. If making additions, check how other wiring has been arranged. Twin cables may go to each point or there may be a single wire, with the switch and fuse on the live side and another wire to a common earth cable.

Earth usually means a cable which serves as

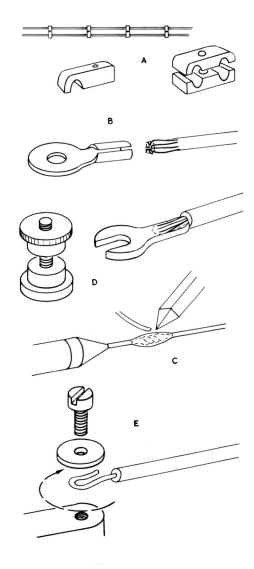

*34. Electric cables may be held by clips (A). End fittings should make good contact (B) and preferably be soldered (D). Twisted wires can be soldered (C). A wire around a screw should be arranged in the direction of tightening (E).*

a return line and does not imply a connection to earth or water, but there could be a connection from it to a keel bolt or other through-hull fitting, and this can be expected to reduce radio interference.

If the existing electrical system in a boat is to be unaltered, it will be advisable to check through all the wiring, especially if you are unfamiliar with it and where it all goes. In an emergency you may be glad to know, for instance, that the wiring to the cabin lamps has been looped behind the casing for the steering cable and goes through a cupboard below the cooker, where there is an inline fuse located. Checking through will also show you if wires have come loose or insulation has been damaged.

Pay particular attention to end connections (fig. 34B). The best connection is soldered as that makes a permanent metal-to-metal through path for the electricity, with no risk of corrosion occurring between the surfaces (fig. 34C). With a screwed terminal (fig. 34D) or a push-in connection, there is a risk that surfaces will corrode and the quality of the connection will deteriorate, possibly not enough to stop the equipment working, but it may not function at its greatest efficiency. If wire is twisted in a loop around the connection screw, go clockwise in the direction of tightening and it is best to encircle the screw completely (fig. 34E). A falling off of efficiency may be gradual and not very apparent, but you will not be getting such good results and your battery is having to work harder.

Many connections on electrical gear are made of commerical brass, which has little resistance to corrosion in a salty atmosphere. If a wire to a screwed connection has corrosion around it, even if it is only a darkening and dulling of the metal, open the joint and clean off the surfaces so they are bright again. Emery cloth can be used around a wire end, but the point of a knife scraped sideways is usually better for getting at the surfaces close in to the screw of the terminal. The battery should be switched off or disconnected while you do this, in case you short the knife across another terminal, causing sparking, the blowing of a fuse or other damage.

To prevent or delay further corrosion, smear the terminal with petroleum jelly or Vaseline or one of the preparations sold by car accessories' firms for use on battery terminals. Joints could be sprayed with one of the preparations such as WD40 intended to keep equipment dry. However, much depends on the situation. Grease or spray may affect the instrument or other item and a spray may affect the clarity of the glass over a dial.

Insulating tape has its uses. Plastic types are better afloat than the older electrician's treated fabric tapes. If a wire has to be extended by joining on a further length, merely twisting the ends together may seem satisfactory at first, but corrosion will start and impair conductivity. The twisted ends could be soldered, staggered in twin cables (fig. 35A), and then wrapped with several thicknesses of tape. Alternatively use screwed connectors of the type where the two ends go into opposing holes and are held by set screws on the side (fig. 35B), with the whole

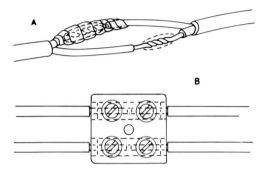

*35. Soldered joints in twin cable should be staggered and bound with insulating tape (A). Joints are best made in insulated screwed connectors (B).*

be well looked after. This book is not concerned with the boat's main or auxiliary motor, which will almost certainly provide charging for the battery. An alternator is better than a dynamo, as it will charge adequately at idling speed and bring a low battery back into full life more quickly. The charging leads should be stout and no longer than necessary. Do not be tempted to resite the battery some way from the alternator, as this would result in a fall-off of charging efficiency.

thing enclosed in a semi-flexible plastic case. These are cheap and better than the push-in connectors used in some cars; wrap the connector with tape after making the connection. In general, it is better to carry one wire right through than to join two separate lengths, but there will have to be branches and proper junction boxes are the correct things for arranging these.

Electric wiring should be kept at least four feet from a boat's steering compass, but if a twin cable has to run close to it, twist the wires round each other. This will reduce interference with magnetism.

## Batteries

As the battery is the source of power and your electrical system is useless without it, it should

### Dynamo or alternator

Newer engines usually have an alternator, which produces alternating current to be rectified for battery charging, but older installations have a dynamo, producing direct current and using a voltage regulator. Both types are normally belt driven, as they are in a car, and there is an adjustment to take up belt slack. There should be a small amount of play in the belt. How much depends on its length, but a sideways movement of 20mm ($\frac{3}{4}$in) between pulleys is about right. Apart from this adjustment and checking the electrical connections to external wiring, there are no other checks to the alternator.

A dynamo should also be checked occasionally for belt tension and good external electrical connections, but there are a few other things that may be looked at by the owner. Noise may come from loose mounting bolts or worn bearings, which would have to be replaced by an expert. Erratic charging could be caused by a carefully (fig. 36A) and put it somewhere clean. The armature assembly can then be pulled out of the body.

Look at the commutator (the reduced end divided into segments). Wipe it clean with a cloth lightly moistened with petrol. The grooves between the segments should be clear. Use a pin to stroke lightly along each groove (fig. 36B), and make sure all particles of dirt are removed with the cloth. If the commutator surface is obviously badly worn or pitted, a piece of glass-paper can be used around it. Do not use emery cloth, which might leave conducting particles. If damage is bad, overhaul must be by a specialist. Finally clean with the cloth moistened with petrol, changing to a new clean part of it.

The brushes are on the end plate and are held against the commutator by springs. Unscrew the terminal and withdraw the wire and carbon brush. Check the action of the spring: if it has lost temper, shown by change of colour, or is obviously weak, change it. If the existing equipment seems satisfactory, clean the guides with cloth moistened with petrol and re-assemble. Otherwise, fit new parts. The carbon brushes will be square sided, but the end will be curved where it lies in contact with the revolving commutator. If it is worn right down, replace; otherwise see that it is re-assembled in its natural sense and not at right angles.

To allow re-assembly, the brushes have to be kept back clear of the commutator. Lift the springs and hook them over the guides, so they do not press on the brushes. Pull the brushes back. Slide the parts together, bringing the end

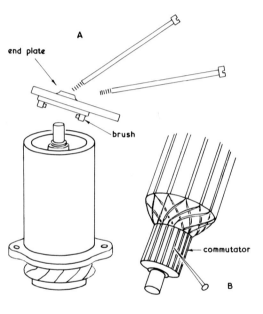

36. *Removing the end plate of a dynamo (A) allows dismantling so the commutator can be serviced (B).*

poor earth connection but, if you suspect the trouble is internal or charging actually ceases, it is possible to open the dynamo and attend to sticking brushes, weak springs or a dirty or burned commutator. Details vary between makes, but dismantling and attention are broadly as follows.

External electrical connections are undone, bolts and the driving belt are removed and the dynamo lifted out. The end plate, opposite to the pulley end, is held with long bolts, which can be turned with a screwdriver. Pull it off plate gently into place with the brushes clear. Fit the long retaining bolts that hold the parts together, but do not tighten them excessively. Put a thin screwdriver through the access holes in the end plate and ease the springs into position to press the brushes against the commutator. Test the rotation of the dynamo and mount it in position with the driving belt correctly tensioned.

Do not be tempted to lubricate during assembly. The bearing at the pulley end is pre-packed with lubricant and no more should be added there. At the end plate there may be a lubricating point, and a small amount of light lubricating oil can be added here at long intervals. Oil getting on to electrical parts can cause trouble.

If there are signs of overheating, when the dynamo is opened, such as solder thrown about, there is nothing that can be done except pass the work to an expert, and then it will probably be simplest to get a replacement dynamo. If it is a car type, the makers may offer an exchange arrangement.

In most boats the battery is of the lead/acid type, similar to that used in cars. If you are replacing a battery, it may be worthwhile getting one the same as in your car. It will then be possible to switch with the batteries in the car, so both are charged and used and maintained in good condition, even during a period when the boat is laid up. The alternative, if boat use is infrequent, is to take the battery ashore and keep it topped up with a trickle charger at intervals. A lead/acid battery will

deteriorate if left for a long period in a partly discharged state.

An alternative to the car-type battery is one made up of nickel/cadmium alkali cells (Nife). These cost more, but they have a very long life and will stand up to abuse and neglect better. Leaving them partly discharged may not matter and they can be recharged at a higher rate than would be advisable for lead/acid batteries.

Another newer alternative is the maintenance-free battery, which is the same as a lead/acid battery for practical purposes, but it is sealed and never needs attention, other than charging.

The cells in a lead/acid battery each produce an average of 2 volts, so there are six cells in the usual 12-volt battery, but in use the voltage may drop to 1·8 volts or soar to 2·2 volts, and equipment must suit the range 10·8 to 13·2 volts for a nominal 12 volt output. The cells in a nickel/cadmium battery are only about 1·4 volts, so for 12-volt equipment there have to be eight or nine of them.

A lead/acid battery contains an acid, the water content of which gases off during charging. Topping up should be with distilled water, although an occasional use of tap water, if there is nothing else, does not seem to matter and would be better than leaving the acid level low. Boiling the tap water and allowing it to cool would be better than using it direct. The acid level may be marked on the case. If not, it should be enough to cover the plates, which are visible through the filler holes. Do not overdo it. A container with a spout having a plastic valve in its end is a good thing for carrying topping-up

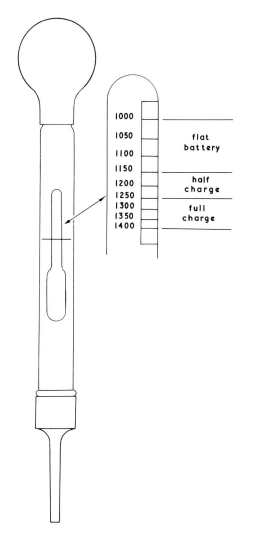

| | |
|---|---|
| 1000 | |
| 1050 | flat |
| 1100 | battery |
| 1150 | |
| 1200 | half |
| 1250 | charge |
| 1300 | full |
| 1350 | charge |
| 1400 | |

water and a means of ensuring it is cut off before too much goes in. Never introduce fresh acid.

*Charging*

The state of charge is best checked by testing the specific gravity of the acid in each cell and this is done with a hydrometer–a float that gives the reading is enclosed in a glass tube with a small hose to go in the cell and a bulb at the top to suck up acid (plate 17). If you have topped up with water, let the battery go on charging for some time before testing, otherwise you will suck up water or weaker acid from the top and not get a correct reading. When you suck up acid there may be coloured balls that either float or do not float to indicate the charge. Check the meaning of the colours on the instrument or its case. The more scientific instrument has a float calibrated to indicate the specific gravity of the acid (fig. 37). It may also have coloured markings to give a quick guide to the state of charge. In a fully charged battery the reading for each cell should be between 1·250 and 1·270. There may be variations between cells, but if these are not great, they will not matter. If one or more cells is consistently different from the others, your battery may be nearing the end of its life. Many car batteries can only be expected to last about two years, and intermittent use coupled with periods of partial discharge may shorten life further in a boat.

*37. The float in a hydrometer shows the specific gravity of the acid drawn up by squeezing the bulb.*

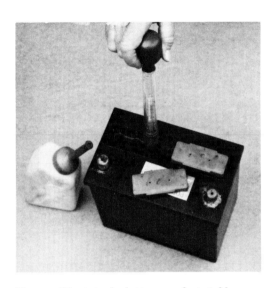

*Plate 17. The state of a battery may be tested by checking the specific gravity of the acid in each cell with a hydrometer. A container of topping-up water alongside has a valve to prevent overfilling.*

Connections to most batteries are via lead posts standing above the end cells. Make connections with the same sort of connectors that are used in cars; these have an all-round tight grip and a good area of contact. Avoid spring clip or alligator connectors, which may be satisfactory for temporary connections, as when a trickle charger is used or for getting a car going with jump leads from another battery, but they have insufficient area of contact for long use. There will be sulphation, or corrosion, if you do nothing about it, so scrape contacts clean and coat with a protective jelly.

A battery will 'gas'. This may not be much, but the gas should be given a path of escape. Do not seal the battery in a closed casing if it is connected to a charger and preferably vent any cover to the outside of the boat. If the battery does not get charged in the boat, but has to be taken ashore for charging, it could be in a closed box with a carrying handle, possibly with the boat wiring plugged into the outside of the box (plate 18). Boxes and plugs and sockets are sold for caravan use and could be adapted.

Batteries are heavy and could affect the trim of the boat. They must be securely anchored in their stowage, or else violent movement of the boat may cause them to become dislodged; and in cases of a boat suffering a complete knock-down, an unsecured battery could injure the crew and put the engine out of action. Although weight ought to be kept low and central if possible, batteries (particularly metal-cased alkaline ones) should be away from bilge water. Traditional battery trays have been made of wood and lined with rubber or pitch, but there are several plastics that are unaffected by battery liquids. An industrial plastic tray or even a rectangular plastic bowl might be adapted; see that it has a lid with air holes. If a traditional tray needs refurbishing, bitumastic paint can be used inside. Battery acid will destroy cloth, even if it is only spray or vapour, so do not leave a battery exposed where clothing might touch it. Remember the risk of acid attacking cloth when putting away the hydro-meter. Squirt the acid back into each cell as it is tested, then run clear water through the instru-

*Plate 18. If the battery is portable and taken ashore for charging, it may fit in a box with a socket outside.*

regulator. On the side that serves lighting and other needs in the boat there is sometimes nothing to provide protection. There should be a switch in the live line or preferably a double pole switch that isolates the battery completely from the circuit.

Switches further along the system should be in the live line. The system connected to the engine is earthed on one side; negative earth (−) is usual, but check the actual installation. The other or positive (+) line is the live side and must be the one switched on the domestic side. This also applies to fuses; if they are put in the earth side of the system they will be ineffective.

Be warned: if the system is charged by an alternator, *never* isolate the battery while the engine is running, even to switch rapidly to another battery. You will blow the alternator. When leaving the boat, turn off the isolating switch; even if no electrical equipment is left on, there will be a slow drain through the wiring.

## Lighting

Most interior lighting is effected by car-type bulbs, and similar bulbs are often used for deck and spreader lights. The common type are described as SBC, meaning small bayonet caps, and these can be 18mm, 25mm and 38mm ($\frac{3}{4}$, 1 and $1\frac{1}{2}$in). BC stands for bayonet cap and indicates full-size caps. Low voltage and the limited capacity of the battery necessitates the use of low-wattage bulbs and the smallest size

ment before putting it away empty. Do not merely put it down, where acid from the end may cause damage. There could be a compartment for the hydrometer alongside the battery tray, but make sure it is kept clean. Dirt from its end should not be introduced to the battery.

If the same battery is used for engine starting, the circuits on that side of the system will be protected with a cutout and charging voltage of 5 watts is common. In the smaller cabins this gives adequate, if not brilliant, lighting. If alterations using these bulbs are considered, economy with a reasonable spread of light comes from having several lamps, possibly each with its own switch and a master switch at the door.

Even if bulbs of higher wattage are used, the light should not be restricted by complicated shades. Decorative and enclosing shades limit what is already not a very bright light. As with household lamps, these small bulbs may fall off in efficiency with age. If the glass shows signs of darkening, a new bulb should be tried in its place.

Although a higher wattage bulb might be tried, the drain on the battery has to be considered and a way to get a brighter cabin light without using more electricity is to change at least some of the lights to fluorescent. Like mains fluorescent lights, these are long and there must be space to accommodate them, but the light value is considerably more than a normal bulb of the same wattage. Most of these lamp fittings are almost completely made of plastic, so there should be no corrosion problem except at the contacts, which should be looked at annually. Most makes are available in 8 watt and 13 watt, or there may be a version with two 8-watt lamps side-by-side. A 12-volt 8-watt fluorescent lamp is claimed to have a light output equal to a 40-watt domestic lamp, and a 13 watt one is equal to 60 watt.

Typical overall sizes of fittings are:

8 watt–350mm by 45mm by 35mm
($14$in $\times$ $1\frac{3}{4}$in $\times$ $1\frac{3}{8}$in)

13 watt–570mm by 45mm by 35mm
($22$in $\times$ $1\frac{3}{4}$in $\times$ $1\frac{3}{8}$in)

Fluorescent lamp fittings usually incorporate a switch. The lamp has to be connected the right way, so read the installation instructions. If polarity is reversed, it will not work, or could be damaged, although most lamp fittings are now protected so you can put right a mistake without the unit suffering. They interfere with D/F equipment, so it is best to switch them off when taking radio bearings.

Switches for use with 12-volt equipment should be of a type intended for use afloat. Normal domestic mains type could be used, but watch out for some rather basic switches that may be satisfactory in caravans, but which have no place on a boat.

The lighting circuits will almost certainly serve navigation, spreader and other outside lights. As these are more vulnerable than inside lighting, they should be of marine type and not adaptations of inside or caravan types. With the battery disconnected, go around the light fittings and take out the bulbs in turn. Scrape bright the contacts in the sockets and on the bulb caps. Be careful not to leave scrapings where they may cause a short. A cloth moistened with methylated spirits can be wrapped around a finger and used to get out metal particles.

Some navigation lamps have festoon bulbs, which rely for good contact on sprung supports against their metal ends. Besides cleaning the contacts, bend the ends to tighten them, if necessary. Check rubber sealing when replacing covers. A smear of jointing compound can be

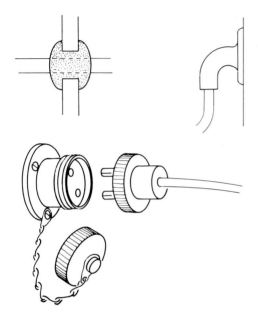

*38. Cable through a cabin side should be watertight.*
*Any external plug and socket should be a marine type.*

put on the rubber. Use the type that never fully hardens, rather than one that sets hard and may make later dismantling difficult. Check where wiring goes through deck or cabin for water-proofness (fig. 38).

There should be fuses in all lighting circuits, but they are particularly important with outside lighting. Check these for their location and satisfactory condition. In an ideal layout the fuses are all at a central control panel and are clearly marked. If your electrical system falls

short of this, check the location of all fuses and make sure you know what they serve. Either mark the fuse panel so you know which circuit each fuse serves, or make a diagram showing the situation of each fuse in the boat, then put the diagram on the inside of the door of a locker or somewhere else where it can be seen and not removed. Someone else may have to trouble-shoot in a hurry when you are unavailable. If a variety of fuses are needed, keep spares packaged in containers marked with their applications, or there could be confusion.

## Other equipment

One electrical device you might consider adding is a converter to allow a normal mains electric razor to be used. This converts 12 volts DC from the battery to 230 volts AC at the usual type of socket for an electric razor. Output is adequate for the purpose, but the unit is not intended for a heavier load, so don't try hooking up the cassette-recorder or you will blow the converter.

If a gas-and-electric refrigerator is installed and the facility for running off 12 volts is to be used, there are several points to watch. The usual small refrigerator has an 85-watt heating element. This is only intended for use while the battery is being charged from a running engine. If the refrigerator is being used electrically while the battery is not receiving a charge, most normal car-size batteries would be flattened in less than 30 minutes. This means that such a system should only be used while the boat is under way and the battery must be disconnected from the refrigerator when the engine is stopped. To allow for this there should be a fuse and switch in the live wire. The smallest refrigerator takes at least a 7 ampère load in the wiring, so the wires should be stouter than those used for lighting and kept as short as possible. Even with a switch for the refrigerator, there is a risk of forgetting to use it, so the battery is drained. If the engine is started with a car-type ignition switch, there is a relay device to fit in the circuit with it, so when the engine is switched off the refrigerator is also.

## Mains electricity

If a boat is moored where shore mains supply can be connected, there may be separate circuits to allow for the use of mains voltage lighting, and this could allow for sockets for heaters and vacuum cleaners to be plugged in. Whether this is worthwhile depends on how much time is to be spent alongside a power supply, as the equipment cannot be used when away from it. The alternative is to convert the mains supply to 12 volts, so the same things are powered from the shore supply as are operated from the battery. The high mains voltage is also potentially dangerous in the proximity of water, so safety precautions and the use of correctly wired outlets are very important. If the mains 220 volts are converted to 12 volts, the only high risk potential is in the cable from the shore outlet to the converter.

Battery chargers are converters, but the numbers of ampères available at the outlet are only sufficient for battery charging at a moderate rate and may only be 3 or 4 ampères at the most, so a battery charger is no use for operating 12-volt equipment from the shore mains–not even one small lamp. It might be possible to continue using the battery while it is charging from one of these units, but more would be drawn out than was being put in.

The size of a mains converter for running 12-volt equipment direct from it governs what is possible. One measuring 180mm by 187mm by 128mm (7in × 7½in × 5in) has a 220 volt input and a 12 volt 16 ampère output, so it would run a 12-volt refrigerator (7 ampères) with power to spare for one light or other appliance. A larger unit might run all the electric services on the boat and would be justified if much time was spent at a marina or elsewhere that power was available.

The mains cable from the shore should be of a substantial type to withstand chafing and it should be regularly inspected. A shock in a wet situation from leaking insulation would be lethal. At the boat end the connection should preferably be in a sheltered place, which would not be splashed or rained on, and the parts should be intended for marine use, not domestic plugs and sockets. A possibly better way of dealing with the connection would be to have the cable direct from the converter through a watertight grommet in a cabin side, with sufficient length to reach the shore outlet. The only snag would then be the need to coil the cable outside, possibly in a locker or a sheltered part of the wheelhouse.

A converter needs no special servicing, other than the cleaning of connections and the replacement of fuses. Usually there is a fuse on the input side and one in each of the outlets. If a fuse blows, locate the cause of trouble before fitting another one.

| Number of wires/ Diameter in inches | Current rating in amperes |
|---|---|
| 1/·004 | 5 |
| 3/·029 | 5 |
| 3/·036 | 10 |
| 1/·064 | 10 |
| 7/·029 | 15 |
| 7/·036 | 24 |
| 7/·044 | 31 |
| 7/·052 | 37 |

Table 2.
Current ratings for copper electrical cables

# ten

# Safety and security equipment

Besides such things as lifebuoys and lifejackets, there are other not so obvious things related to the safety of the crew. There should be precautions taken below decks to minimise accidents. The obvious danger is fire, but there are risks of mishap due to movement of the boat. Allied with safety is the need to secure individual items of equipment and the enclosed part of the boat as a whole, against burglary and vandalism. Although some of the requirements are taken care of in the general design of the boat and its equipment, it is a seamanlike precaution to view the interior with regard to safety and security aspects as first considerations.

## Fire extinguishers

There is not much maintenance to be done by the private owner to existing fire extinguishers. Security of mounting can be checked and the appliances should be cleaned periodically. At the same time it is a good idea to refresh your memory by reading the operating instructions. In an emergency you do not want to have to waste time reading how to use the thing. In many craft the provision of fire extinguishers is inadequate. There may be a feeling that with all that water around there is no need for fire extinguishers, but water must not be used on electrical fires, because of short circuiting and the risk of shock. Water will get underneath instead of on top of burning oil. A fire needs oxygen to continue burning and it is extinguished by smothering it so it is starved of oxygen. Water may kill a general fire by smothering and cooling it, but as most fires on board involve electricity or oil, something else is preferable.

A water-filled extinguisher can usually be checked by unscrewing the cap. Inside is a phial of acid that will be broken when the knob is pressed; this can be checked visually. The main part of the extinguisher should be found almost full of water. In fact it is water with sodium carbonate mixed with it. It is the reaction of the acid with this that generates a gas to force the water out. If the container is empty or only partly full, it is no use topping up with water only. The maker should be asked to service the extinguisher.

Most other extinguishers cannot be checked easily. Some types are marked with a weight when they are in working order, so that leakage can then be checked by weighing. Others have their life marked on them and should be regarded as suspect after expiry. Ideally, extinguishers that cannot be checked should be mounted in pairs, to give a second chance, but space may preclude that although it may be possible to change extinguishers at staggered dates, so all are not the same age.

The specialist firms dealing with fire extinguishers will advise on particular installations. It is possible to hire, instead of buy, some extinguishers on a maintenance contract, so you get a check on the state of the extinguisher at least annually. They will also check your own extinguishers. When dealing with what could be a matter of life or death, it is advisable to bring in the experts.

*Plate 19. A small BCF fire extinguisher has clear instructions on the outside, but it is wise to familiarise yourself with them before any emergency arises.*

When preparing to install new fire extinguishers it is advisable to choose those that are suitable for all kinds of fire on board. You cannot be selective and water from over the side should only be regarded as a follow-up on burning wood or cloth, but in the first attack you want an extinguisher that can be directed anywhere, whether there is burning fuel, wood or fibreglass, or electrical gear that is still alive.

Foam extinguishers are used ashore on oil and petrol fires in particular, but the amount of foam generated and the difficulty of removing it all afterwards, make another type preferable for boat use. Carbon dioxide ($CO_2$) extinguishers serve a similar purpose without the mess and are electrically non-conductive. Another type gives a high-speed jet for rapid action and contains bromochlorodifluoromethane, normally and understandably usually described as BCF (plate 19). Dry foam extinguishers smother the fire with a powder. At one time many extinguishers were filled with carbon-tetra-chloride (CTC), which is effective at extinguishing a fire, but the fumes are extremely toxic and dangerous in a confined space. It is advisable to ventilate thoroughly any compartment after an extinguisher has been used. As oxygen has been removed and gas left in the compartment, going into an unventilated space could be dangerous to life.

There is some official advice on fire extinguishers to use as a guide. For vessels up to 9 metres (30ft) length and shorter craft with powerful engines necessitating large quantities of fuel, there should be two extinguishers, each not less than 1·4 kilos (3 lb) capacity, dry powder or equivalent and one or more additional extinguishers of not less than 2·3 kilos (5 lb) capacity, dry powder or equivalent. A fixed installation may be necessary.

For vessels shorter than this, with cooking facilities and engines, the two 1·4 kilo extinguishers described above should be carried. If the vessel has cooking facilities only or engine only, one of the 1·4 kilo extinguishers should be carried.

Also officially advised are two buckets with lanyards for getting water from over the side, and a bag of sand, which is useful in containing and extinguishing burning spillage of fuel or oil, but not particularly practical afloat.

An inboard engine may be hidden, so a fire developing may not be immediately obvious. There are automatic extinguishers to mount in or near the engine compartment. Extra heat at a sensing head activates the extinguisher. These are BCF types and require the same checks as similar portable extinguishers. If there is a remotely controlled extinguisher system with discharge nozzles at the engine and fuel compartments, a check of the piping is needed as well as the container, and operation of the lever or handle can be tried with the container disconnected.

If a flammable vapour warning system is installed, its functioning can be checked by intentionally introducing gas near the sensing head; this could be a cup of bottled gas or a small amount of petrol allowed to vaporise. If the same device includes a warning of bilge water level, that could be induced locally as well. There should be sound and lamp warnings. It is inadvisable to open the device, but there should be an arrangement for adjusting by screw or knob on the outside. A test switch or button proves that the device has functioning lights or bell, but an occasional test at the sensing head checks that it and its connecting wiring are effective.

A possible galley fire is the ignition of fat in a pan. If the pan has a fitting lid, that will extinguish it, but it is a sensible precaution to have a fire blanket within reach of the cook. This is effective and without the mess and fumes of any other sort of extinguisher. Some blankets are made of asbestos fibre, but recent ones are flexible woven glass, which can be washed. A useful size is about 90cm (3ft) square, but it stows in a container 28cm (11in) high and 8cm (3in) square, which can be mounted on a bulkhead or shelf for instant withdrawal. Do not fit it behind the cooker where it cannot be reached if the flames are leaping from a pan.

**Fire precautions**

Location of fire extinguishers need some thought. While they may be put ready for action at the sites of potential fires, they have to be accessible, preferably from inside and outside. The cabin entrance is often near the engine compartment, where a fire might prevent the extinguisher being reached. There should be a second access to a cabin, possibly through a deck hatch, and one extinguisher might be better positioned there, where it could be reached from inside or outside.

If fire risks are kept in mind when choosing cabin equipment, the possibilities of a conflagration can be reduced. Carried to its logical conclusion, if everything in the boat is fireproof, there is no need for extinguishers. Obviously that cannot be, but where there is a choice of flammable or non-flammable items,

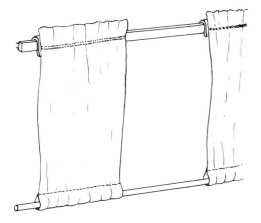

*39. If a curtain has to slide near a cooker, its bottom should be sleeved on a rod.*

other things being equal, the choice is obvious.

Metals do not burn, but many things that were metal are now plastic. Fortunately, many modern plastics will not burn. Some may melt instead of burn, while others are unaffected, at least until the heat gets very intense. There is no way of discovering whether a plastic item is liable to burn or not by examination, so we have to rely on what the makers say.

Curtains and other cloths may be natural or synthetic fibres. Nearly all will burn. Some synthetics will dissolve first, but it does not take much heat to cause them to burst into flames. In some small cruisers with hotplate cookers in the cabin, curtains may pull back dangerously close to them. Elsewhere it may be satisfactory to tie them back, but here it would

be better to eliminate them if possible, but if not, curtains would be better provided with a hem and rod at the bottom (fig. 39) so they cannot flap near the flames.

The makers of proofing solutions for cloth and canvas include fireproofing as well as rot-proofing and waterproofing in some solutions. These are particularly intended for tents, but a clear fireproofing solution can be used on fabrics in a cabin. For things like fabric bunk cushions, this double proofing gives protection against spilled drinks and other liquids as a bonus to fireproofing. If light fabrics, such as curtains, are washed, fireproofing will have to be repeated each time.

Wood can also be treated with a fireproofing solution, but this has to be done before it is given any surface treatment. Protection time depends on penetration and is limited, but anything that retards burning must be a benefit. Surprisingly, wood is not such a fire hazard as might be expected. Paint on it may rapidly ignite, but it takes a considerable conflagration alongside it to do more than make most hard-woods do more than char. The resinous soft-woods are exceptions. Pitch pine, for instance, is full of inflammable resin.

## Personal safety

Most cabins contain a multiplicity of projections against which persons may knock as the boat rolls and pitches. In a well-found boat it should be possible to move from handhold to handhold in rough conditions, so there is a reduced risk of falling or sliding. The cabin sole should be level throughout if possible but, if there has to be a step, it should be obvious to avoid tripping and there should be handholds close. One of the synthetic carpet materials that is unaffected by damp makes a good non-slip floor covering.

Any parallel edges, whether plywood or thicker solid wood, can be converted to hand grips with half-round moulding (fig. 40A). A plywood edge might have a hole cut through it and its edges rounded (fig. 40B) or this incorporated with a moulded grip (fig. 40C).

Any handles provided must be securely attached. There could be the whole weight of a falling person to support and a failed attachment could make an accident worse. Shaped wood handles (fig. 40D) look and feel better than metal ones, but bolt right through and have large washers the other side to prevent the bolts pulling into the wood (fig. 40E). There could be a rail where something longer than a handle may be located. So long as it does not interfere with headroom it could go lengthwise under the cabin top. It might be in a position where it could also be used by anyone getting into or out of a bunk. There are metal fittings to take round rods (fig. 41A) or a flatter piece can be held off by packings (fig. 41B).

A small cabin may be made to seem more roomy by avoiding divisions. There may be only part of a bulkhead to mark the limit of the galley or a navigation table. A disadvantage of this open plan is that the several steps needed to get from one end to the other may be without anything to hold. The edge of a part bulkhead

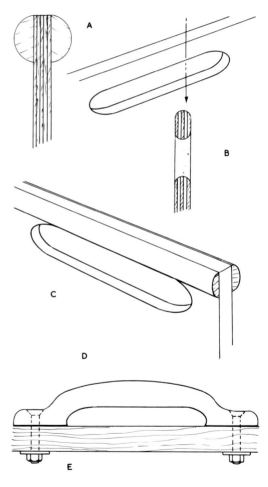

40. *Handholds can be made by thickening (A), by holes (B) or both (C). A wooden handle (D) can have the load taken by large washers (E).*

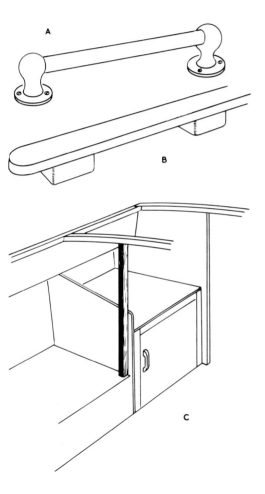

41. A grab handle can be made with a wooden rod in
metal fittings (A) or built up with wood blocks (B). A
part bulkhead can have a post upwards for grabbing (C).

can be taken up to the cabin top with a post
(fig. 41C) that is well rounded. Besides offering
something to grab, it may give extra stiffening
to the cabin top.

You can remain in a bunk in rough conditions by using bunk boards, but the boards
are bulky to stow when out of use. In a small
cabin boat, where the bunks are settees during
the day, something that will stow more com-
pactly is needed. It is possible to use a line
around half cleats under the bunk front to
others on the cabin top. The line might go
through holes in a strip of wood instead of
around cleats (fig. 42A). Several strands of rope
against the body may not be very comfortable
and canvas could be included, fixed to the bunk
front and with eyelets for the rope (fig. 42B).
When out of use the canvas goes under the bunk
cushion. In both cases there is no need to go to
the full length of the bunk–from the chest to the
thighs should be enough. It would then be
possible to get out in emergency without the
need to undo knots.

The variety of cabin tables seems infinite.
Everyone who builds a boat seems to have his
own ideas about table design. In a rolling boat,
or even one moored in a river and subject to
wash from passing craft, the table should have
fiddles. They need not be very high, but they
should come a short distance above the edge of
the deepest dish to be used. If the table top can
be turned over, the fiddles may be permanent
on one side, then the table turned over if they
are not needed or charts are to be spread out.
If fiddles are needed it is because conditions

are such that liquids may be spilled. Consequently they should be arranged so the table can be
wiped off. This is best done by having open
corners and probably gaps in their length.

Fiddles that can be removed may have dowel
rod plugs (fig. 42C). Shape the fiddles like hand
grips, but there is no need to round the cut-
outs. Glue the dowels into the fiddles. Round
their ends and reduce them slightly by rubbing
around with glasspaper. Do not try to get the
holes evenly spaced around the table edge. It is
just about impossible to arrange things so that
the parts are interchangeable. Instead, it is
better to stagger the spacing deliberately, so
one part only goes in one place and only one
way round (fig. 42D). If much food preparation
is done under way, a webbing body-strap with
firm anchorage points should be provided for
the cook.

## Security

Unfortunately, if anyone wants to burgle your
boat there is really no way you can prevent him.
All you can do is make it so difficult that he will
not persist in his efforts. In most cases, if what
he wants to steal cannot be obtained quickly,
he will not spend a long time trying to get it,
with the increased risk of being detected.

Part of the care and maintenance of your

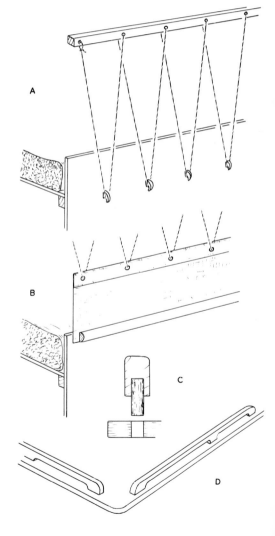

*42. Rope can be used to keep you in a bunk (A), or
this can be used with canvas (B). Removable table
fiddles can have dowels into holes (C) and staggered
positions ensure correct locations.*

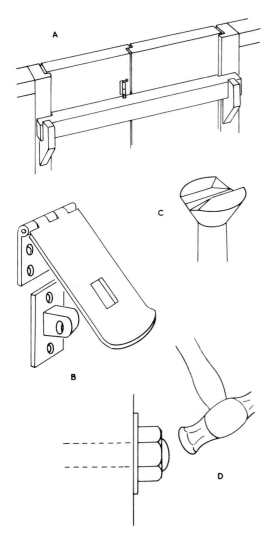

boat should be a check of its internal security. Are hatch fastenings secure and impossible to operate from outside? Is the door lock tamper-proof? Bolts and fastenings should be intended for use afloat. Many door bolts and locks used ashore have steel that will rust or common brass that will corrode. In particular, a lock that rusts inside may frustrate your attempts to open it, as well as those of a thief.

Double doors are particularly vulnerable. One door should bolt at top and bottom and the other door lock to it. If the doors come under a sliding hatch, so the first door cannot be bolted at the top, there may be a bar across both doors inside, which can be positioned before the hatch is pulled along (fig. 43A).

Sliding hatches move in several ways. With some, anyone knowing the design would not have much difficulty in breaking away the runners so the hatch could be lifted off. See that yours is secure. Where the sliding hatch and door meet the usual method of locking is with a hasp and staple. This is satisfactory providing the screw heads are covered when the lock is in place (fig. 43B). It is unwise to use wood screws. There should be bolts through to nuts inside. If any slotted head is still exposed, it can be made one-way by filing away the edges of the screwdriver slot in the direction of undoing (fig. 43C); this does not interfere

*43. Double cabin doors may be reinforced with a bar inside (A). A hasp and staple should cover the screw heads (B). Filing the edges of a screwdriver slot will prevent undoing (C). A bolt end can be spread over a nut to prevent it being unscrewed (D).*

with driving. On the other side the end of the bolt can be spread over the nut, so it cannot be removed (fig. 43D).

Warning devices are mostly adaptations of those intended for household use, and many parts will not stand up to damp conditions. They all need electricity, and a 12-volt battery does not have the power to bring on high-powered lights nor operate a loud horn for long. As the burglar may be trying to break in because the boat is moored some way from habitations, such frightening noises and lights your system can produce may not deter him. Beware of false confidence.

Obviously these systems have some uses, but it is better to remove temptation by taking portable valuable items ashore. Making entry obviously difficult is one deterrent, but the best precaution is to have the boat where it is either under supervision or in good view of other people. Chain instead of rope for moorings, loose items removed from the deck and cockpit, running rigging reduced to the essentials and properly secured, compass and winch-handles removed below, all give an impression of a properly-secured ship, so a would-be thief may think your boat is not worth further attention.

## Personal buoyancy

What you wear to keep you afloat if you find yourself in the water is obviously of prime importance, and should be kept in first-class condition and replaced if it is defective. A lifejacket or buoyancy aid that is faulty should not

be kept on board. In emergency it could inspire false confidence and be dangerous.

In Britain a lifejacket has to satisfy certain conditions of the British Standards Institute, including being able to turn an unconscious person face-up; approved lifejackets carry the BSI kitemark. Less bulky are buoyancy aids, which are approved by the Ship and Boat Builders' National Federation, but they are not as buoyant and it is assumed that the wearer is able to help himself. Solid buoyant material in modern aids is plastic foam. In the most recent types it is closed-cell foam, which does not absorb water. Other foam is like a sponge and can soak up enough water to become ineffective. Buoyancy by inflation may be air or $CO_2$.

An early buoyant material was kapok–a vegetable fibre. Modern thought is against its use and any jackets using this that are on board should be put ashore. This also applies to certain inflatable belts and cushion-type jackets that were available before research discredited them.

Check the overall construction of a jacket or aid. Look at stitching, particularly of straps and fasteners (plates 20 and 21). Try a jacket on and see that it fits and is secure. An oversize one can be dangerous for a child, as it would float up. Buying bigger to allow for a child growing into it is not a safe policy for selecting a lifejacket.

Where open-cell foam has been used, each piece should be sealed in a waterproof bag. It may not be possible to extract and examine

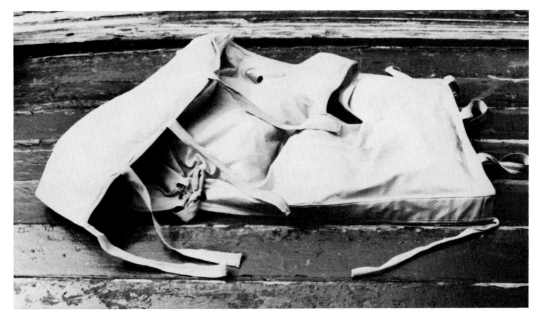

*Plate 20. A waistcoat-pattern buoyancy aid may depend on its fit and the security of the tape fastenings. Its casing should be unbroken and the user should understand how to tie with reef bows.*

this, but feeling through the outer cover will show if it is intact. Check the outer covering for snags and holes (plate 22). Water that gets in is very difficult to remove, even if it does not affect the foam inside.

If mouth inflation is used, blow up the garment and leave it for a few hours to check that it will hold air. If it goes down, even slightly, immerse the garment in water and look for tell-tale bubbles. Most approved garments are made of rubberised fabric and a hole may be patched in the same way as a bicycle inner tube. The material must be dry. Sand around the puncture just before patching. A tyre patch could be used, but it might be neater to use similar material to that used for the jacket. Put rubber solution on the jacket and the patch, then leave to dry. Put on a second coat and leave to get tacky, then press together. French chalk can follow to remove stickiness from excess solution around the patch. If the patch is rectangular, round its corners to reduce any tendency to curl back.

*Plate 21. The tapes of a B.S.I. approved lifejacket are looped around the neck part and are attached to the back of the bottom part. Check all stitching and look for signs of wear.*

Gas inflation is usually by a small $CO_2$ cartridge or cylinder operated by a pull or lever (plate 23). The makers may indicate the life of the cartridge. The weight of a fully-charged cartridge should be marked on it, so its state can be checked by weighing. Unscrewing a cartridge will show if its end has been punctured.

If there is no hole and the weight is correct, the cartridge should still be satisfactory. While the cartridge is unscrewed, operate and test the mechanism. Clean it if necessary. As each cartridge is good for once only, you should carry spares on board and their stowage place should be known to the crew.

Makers of some lifejackets offer an inspection service, so if you have any doubts, return your jackets for inspection. Lifejackets and buoyancy aids should be treated with respect and have a

*Plate 22. The new B.S.I. approved lifejacket on the left, is beside a horrible example that is torn and frayed and should be destroyed.*

safe stowage, possibly in nets. Avoid letting them be used as cushions.

## Harnesses

Safety harnesses are made strongly and they should normally require little maintenance. If a harness has received a shock, possibly by the wearer falling overboard and being pulled along, check stitching in the webbing and chafe where metal parts fit. Doubtful stitching can be reinforced by a few handmade stitches using sail twine, with a sail needle and palm. Tie the twine ends together tightly.

Adjustment is usually with metal or plastic slides. Check their movements and see that they do not slip back after adjusting. Wear or bending may cause slipping. It may be possible to straighten a slide, otherwise it will have to be

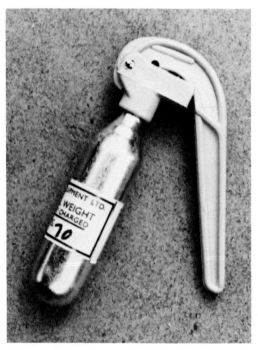

*Plate 23. The vital part of a lifejacket that is $CO_2$ inflated is a small container of gas, that should be marked with its full weight, so its condition can be checked.*

the hinged part. If you decide to replace a line, choose nylon because of the value of its elasticity. From your experience you may find a longer or shorter line would be more use on your boat than the standard length rope.

## Liferafts

Self-inflating liferafts are compulsory for ocean-racing yachts and obviously essential equipment for any craft going far offshore, particularly when any dinghy carried would be inadequate as a lifeboat for the whole crew in bad conditions. The problem of stowage gets worse as the boat gets smaller, and damage may then be more likely. Whether the liferaft is in a flexible valise or a rigid canister, the enemy to watch for is chafe. The best treatment is prevention, by padding. If the valise goes into a deck locker, pad the locker, but do not attach padding to the valise, which would have to be thrown overboard in an emergency.

Opening and repacking a liferaft yourself is not advised. It should be returned to the makers or their authorised agent annually or at the intervals they recommend for their checking and inspection.

replaced. Check the action and security of buckles, particularly the one that takes the strain when the safety line comes under tension.

Examine the safety line for chafe and safe splices. The snap shackles or carbine hooks should give no trouble, but see that they really do snap closed. A little oil may be needed in

## Pyrotechnics

Flares or similar distress signals only become compulsory for craft over 45ft., when not less than six are required, packed in a watertight container, but obviously they are desirable in any smaller craft and essential when going offshore. They are no use if they will not work.

Flares are marked with an expiry date. After that date they should be replaced and may be consigned to a firework display somewhere inland, where their use will not call out the lifeboat! Flares may be waterproof in themselves, but the smaller ones are better in a screwtop plastic container. The best replacement when a group of flares is becoming outdated may be a sealed pack matched to your requirements. Have a safe known stowage so anyone can get at the flares in emergency.

Lights to be thrown overboard with a lifebuoy may be powered by small dry cells. Periodically check the lights and replace batteries, even when there is still some life in them. They may still power a torch, but might not give the intensity of light desirable in a man-overboard light.

## Knock-down

If a boat is knocked down beyond the horizontal, equipment can break loose and fly about, causing injuries which can jeopardise subsequent arrival. Make sure that batteries, spare gas bottles, cookers, heaters, and any heavy item is well secured against the possibility of a 360 degree roll-over. This may sound melodramatic, but experience shows that proper anticipation prevents unwanted drama on the day. Make sure, too, that the main hatch washboards will not fall out when inverted.

# Index